The Reluctant Sheriff

The Reluctant Sheriff

The United States After the Cold War

Richard N. Haass

A COUNCIL ON FOREIGN RELATIONS BOOK

Council on Foreign Relations Books are distributed by Brookings Institution Press (1-800-275-1447). For further information on Council publications, please write the Council on Foreign Relations, 58 East 68th Street, New York, NY 10021, or call the Public Affairs Office at (212 434-9400).

Copyright © 1997 by the Council on Foreign Relations®, Inc.
All Rights Reserved.
Printed in the United States of America.
Fifth Printing 2002

Library of Congress Cataloging-in-Publication Data

Haass, Richard
    The Reluctant Sheriff: The United States After the Cold War/
    Richard N. Haass
        p. cm.
    Includes bibliographical references (p.   ) and index.
    ISBN 0-87609-201-6: $24.95   ISBN 0-87609-198-2: $17.95
        1. United States—Foreign relations—1989–. 2. Cold War.
I. Title.
    E840.H3   1997
    327.73—dc21   97-11422
                                                                  CIP

Contents

To Francesca Maria Beatrice Haass

Introduction

Today's world is different in fundamental ways from the one we knew for 45 years. The Cold War was a relatively structured era of international relations dominated by two great powers and disciplined by nuclear weapons. Rules of the road developed governing competition that reduced the chance the two superpowers would find themselves in direct confrontation involving military forces of any sort. Most other states had their freedom of action circumscribed by their respective superpower patron.

The world in the wake of the Cold War is turning out to be less structured and less disciplined by military force and the fear of nuclear war. It is the age of "deregulation."

The age of deregulation promises to be terribly complex, more so than what came before. For the United States, it is both safer (with no existential Soviet threat) and more dangerous (with the emergence of more numerous if lesser threats). It is more unified and global in the economic and information realms and more discrete and divided in the political. It is better, being more democratic and prosperous for many peoples, and worse, bringing more conflict and poverty for others. Economic, military, and political power will be diffused among a greater number of state and non-state actors than at any time in modern history. All this will occur in a world in which few rules are as yet universally accepted governing behavior within or between states.

1

This is not the same as saying the world will be anarchic. To the contrary, elements of military deterrence will remain in effect. So should many arms control agreements designed to place ceilings on and shape the American and Russian arsenals as well as slow the spread of technology others would need to develop weapons of mass destruction. In addition, numerous institutions and norms affecting important aspects of international activity existed prior to or largely apart from the Cold War; as a result, at the end of the Cold War they are still intact and in some cases more, not less, effective.[1] This applies particularly to the realm of economic affairs, where critical aspects of trade and monetary interaction are regulated in whole or in part.

The other reason the age of deregulation will not be an age of anarchy is the United States. This country emerged from the Cold War, the third great geopolitical contest of the twentieth century, as the single most powerful entity in the world, arguably its only superpower. The United States enjoys a position of primacy—first among *unequals,* if you will—in virtually all spheres, including the military, the economic, and the diplomatic. No other country compares in all three of these areas, and few can compete with the United States in even one.

The ability of the United States to have its way will diminish over time, however. There will no doubt be important exceptions, but the general trend over the long term will be the eroding of U.S. advantage. This erosion will result from two fundamentals: on the one hand, the unavoidable emergence of competing centers of political, economic, and military power; on the other, the avoidable but all the same likely weakening of American will and ability to be an effective world power.

Erosion need not be undesirable. One could argue, for example, that both the Marshall Plan and Japanese reconstruction after World War II were successfully managed cases of eroding U.S. superiority. But too much change, too fast, risks creating a vacuum of authority that could result in all sorts of mayhem. What becomes critical is the speed and extent of any erosion. More than anything else, this will determine how long the age of deregulation endures and whether it is succeeded by an era of anarchy, a renewed Cold War (with China or Russia or both), a multipolar balance among rivals, a concert among like-minded powers such as existed for several decades in post-Napoleonic Europe, an era of democratic peace and prosperity, some combination of the above, or something altogether different. It is not inevitable that things will get worse; the United States, both by what it becomes and how it acts, will have a large impact on how history unfolds.

It will make matters more difficult, though, that the United States will no longer have the luxury of determining whether and how to act in the world on the basis of a dominant threat. As one observer noted, the United States has lost more than an enemy; it has lost the sextant that provided direction for policy.[2] Increasingly, the United States will have to decide what it supports. In such a world there is unlikely to be a neat "solution" to our foreign policy predicament. Any attempt to carry out a "one size fits all" foreign policy will fail.

This is not to suggest that Americans must try to navigate this world without any guide. To the contrary, we should not make such an attempt. It is not enough for a great power to possess a preponderance of strength. It must also have a clarity and soundness of purpose that is understood and supported by its leaders and citizens. A good many vital questions of policy do not lend themselves to ad hoc, short-term approaches. The sizing and shaping of the U.S. armed forces, for example, is a long-term enterprise that must be based on a vision of the world's future and America's purpose within it. The same is true of foreign assistance programs, our intelligence capability, and the training of diplomats. Congress and the public must be educated in the basic tenets of policy if they are to support international undertakings and not run away at the first sign of difficulty or unexpected costs. Just as important, predictability is essential if our allies are going to continue to count on us and not look to themselves or others for their security needs— and if foes are to think twice before challenging U.S. interests. Above all, policymakers acting under the pressure of too little time and too much to do need some bearings by which to judge individual events and their significance if they are not to be swept along by popular emotions, daily headlines, or, increasingly, the latest televised image.

I propose that the United States adopt a foreign policy based on the notion of *regulation*. The United States should act, whenever possible with others but alone when necessary and feasible, to shape the behavior and, in some cases, capabilities of governments and other actors so that they are less likely or able to act aggressively either beyond their borders or toward their own citizens and more likely to enter into trade and other mutually beneficial economic relations. Ideally, multilateral norms, arrangements, and institutions would be developed to help manage international relations. Bringing about such a world, one in which countries settle economic and political disputes peacefully and governments act responsibly toward their own citizens and their neighbors, is the aim of regulation.

A foreign policy of regulation is sure to be too ambitious for some. They will claim that the United States need not concern itself with international developments to such a degree because its interests are few and the threats to them weak, or because we cannot afford such a foreign policy. This last perspective—that the United States simply lacks the resources—stems from the belief that an active foreign policy will prove too expensive and the country must focus its energies and resources at home. It is a central contention of this book that such a belief—one held by some Republicans, Democrats, and independents alike—is both flawed and unwarranted.

As might be expected, a foreign policy of regulation is sure to be too modest for others. Instead, they will want to prolong U.S. dominance by preventing the emergence of rival power centers and/or by seeking to impose American values and preferences on the rest of the world. But such a strategy is simply beyond our means. The effort would bankrupt the United States and, given the growing strength of others, fail, in the process undermining what chance we do have to regulate the behavior of foreign governments and other actors.

For still a third group of observers, a doctrine of regulation is bound to be misguided. They would argue that the focus of policy ought to be different, that the problem is more one of direction than effort. They would oppose an emphasis on interstate relations and favor focusing on promoting human rights and democracy or expanding exports or protecting the environment. I believe that any such emphasis would be ill-advised because other interests must count for more, because we lack leverage, or both—and that a doctrine of regulation is correct to take these interests into account as part of an overall approach but not let any one of them dominate.

My use of terminology with its roots in the marketplace is intentional. Regulation is a concept associated with late-nineteenth and twentieth-century efforts in the United States to protect citizens from the effects of pure capitalism. Such economic Darwinism, it was feared, would lead to the survival of the fittest—another phrase for monopoly or oligopoly power. As a result, the goal of regulation was and is to ensure fair competition. Regulation has taken many forms, including establishing requirements for market entry, setting prices, prohibiting discrimination, and limiting market share. In recent decades, regulation has broadened to protecting investors (often through disclosure requirements), limiting pollution, and establishing safety standards for a wide range of products and activities. The fact that such regulation has gone too far in many instances should not obscure the larger point that some degree of regulation is desirable and necessary. Indeed, even the initiatives of recent years to deregulate various industries such as aviation, trucking, and telecommunications reduce rather than end government involvement in the marketplace.[3]

The concepts of regulation and deregulation are useful in the realm of international relations, which can best be understood as a political, economic, and military marketplace.[4] I say this despite some important differences between the two "markets" and despite the strong and often negative reactions the words "deregulation" and "regulation" produce in some quarters. I use these two words because the former captures the varied and dynamic quality of post–Cold War international relations, while the latter reflects the essence of what I am advocating—a foreign policy that seeks to create more stable relations between governments and other actors in the political, economic, and military arenas.

An added difficulty arises in finding a mechanism for regulation. No "invisible hand" ensures that unstructured interaction will produce peace, prosperity, and morality. To the contrary, history strongly suggests that regulation must be introduced and maintained by "visible" hands if positive things are to emerge or, more modestly, if bad outcomes are to be avoided.

In the domestic marketplace, the federal government constitutes the visible hand and thus the authority of last resort. Obviously, there is no world government. Nor is any country or organization prepared to do more than help. There is only the United States. In the post–Cold War world, in the age of deregulation, the lion's share of the burden of promoting international order falls on the United States. It is a burden worth bearing, both for what can be accomplished and what can be averted.

In many instances, the United States will best be able to do this by assuming the role of international sheriff, one who forges coalitions or posses of states and others for specific tasks. This was the approach used to counter Iraq's aggression against Kuwait. More generally, it makes sense when no organization has the capacity to meet a challenge but when a unilateral or uncoordinated response would be inadequate.

It is important to distinguish between the United States as *sheriff* and the United States as *policeman*. The latter would suggest a greater degree of authority, a greater capacity to act alone, and a greater need to act consistently than is being advocated here. By contrast, a sheriff must understand his lack of clear authority in many instances, his need to work with others, and, above all, the need to be discriminating in where and how he engages.

Moreover, the notion of the United States as sheriff is one derived more from necessity than desirability. It would be much less demanding on Americans if it were not necessary for the sheriff to saddle up with any frequency. A goal of American foreign policy must therefore be to promote the emergence of capable, standing organizations that can share the burden of regulation.

What may prove to be the greatest constraint on the ability of the United States to implement a foreign policy of regulation successfully is its domestic situation. Robert Tucker has framed this question boldly: "The great issue of American foreign policy today . . . is the contradiction between the persisting desire to remain the premier global power and an ever deepening aversion to bear the costs of this position."[5] In reality, the situation is even more complex. There is less interest in and consensus over foreign policy than at any time in the past half-century. For many Americans, the debate is not so much over which foreign policy to adopt as whether to have one at all. Events abroad are increasingly viewed as remote and relatively unconnected to day-to-day concerns or, even worse, a distraction that we as a society can ill afford, given all that is wrong and cries out for attention within our own borders.[6]

That such views are understandable and quite widespread makes them no less wrong or misguided. The United States needs an active foreign policy. Victory in the Cold War did not end either the promise or the danger in the world beyond our borders. New great powers will inevitably arise. When they do, major war is a possibility. Moreover, while no existing threat to us is as great as the old Soviet Union, numerous threats are still posed by terrorists, rogue states, and various cartels that can do enormous damage. The Iraqi invasion of Kuwait, the World Trade Center bombing, the gassing in Japan's subway—all are indications of what could happen on a much larger, more destructive scale. Indeed, what is most surprising is that no such event has taken place, a good fortune we would be foolish to expect to persist.

There is also the fact that the U.S. economy is more integrated with the economies of other states than at any other time. Similarly, we cannot insulate ourselves from environmental change or disease or migration pressures. And there remains the lingering question of values, that we care about people elsewhere in the world just as we care about people in neighboring cities because we are citizens of a common society. In the end, foreign policy is not so foreign.

Conducting a foreign policy of regulation will be costly. It will require a modern military capability, including the capacity to deter the use of force, fight traditional wars, cope with the proliferation of nuclear, biological, and chemical weapons and advanced delivery systems, and deal with lesser but still demanding humanitarian contingencies of the sort posed by Bosnia or Rwanda. Brave men and women will lose their lives carrying out these missions. Policymakers and soldiers will need the support of costly intelligence agencies; no amount of general information can take the place of a government agency dedicated to producing timely and focused analysis. We will need resources to conduct diplomacy—to maintain our missions abroad—and funds to provide adequate assistance to those countries and organizations unable to provide for themselves.

A foreign policy of regulation will also take up time. It will require government officials to make difficult decisions and build domestic and international support for their implementation. It will also require a commitment by our schools, foundations, and media organizations to accord attention to international subjects that they deserve but do not always receive.

The best justification for such expense is that the alternatives—including doing less—are likely to prove more costly in the end. The result would be a world less safe for American interests and less compatible with American values. It is important, also, to keep matters in context. A foreign policy of regulation promises to be affordable. The direct cost of the sort of foreign policy advocated here—on the order of what we are already doing—will not be so great as to have an adverse impact on either our economy or our society.

A foreign policy of regulation will prove less costly and more effective if others are engaged on a realistic basis. This translates into avoiding unilateralism for the most part but also jettisoning highly ambitious schemes for international institutions to manage political and military (as opposed to economic) issues. It requires a willingness to conduct a foreign policy predicated in the first instance on the United States overcoming its reluctance to act, where possible by building lasting arrangements with other states, where necessary by forging informal coalitions of others that are both able and willing to join in.

All this will be difficult. We are talking about a more complicated foreign policy to meet the threats posed by a more complex world at a time when the American people will be less disposed to lend their support. Demands on politicians will rise, because the prerequisite for effective international leadership is responsible domestic leadership. The fact that it will be difficult, however, will hardly shield us from the consequences if we come up short. History tends to be unsparing of societies that fail to meet the challenges they could and should have dealt with when the challenges were still relatively small.

NOTES

1. On this point, see G. John Ikenberry, "The Myth of Post–Cold War Chaos," *Foreign Affairs* 75, no. 3 (May/June 1996), 79–91.
2. C. William Maynes, "America Without the Cold War," *Foreign Policy*, no. 78 (Spring 1990), 5.
3. For background on the concepts of regulation and deregulation as used in the traditional sense, see Stephen Breyer, *Regulation and Its Reform* (Cambridge, Mass.: Harvard University Press, 1982); Martha Derthick and Paul J. Quirk, *The Politics of Deregulation* (Washington, D.C.: Brookings, 1985); and James Q. Wilson (ed.), *The Politics of Regulation* (New York: Basic Books, 1980).
4. For a scholarly treatment of such ideas, see Morton A. Kaplan, *System and Process in International Politics* (New York: John Wiley & Sons, 1957).
5. Robert W. Tucker, "The Future of a Contradiction," *National Interest*, no. 43 (Spring 1996), 20.
6. For useful background in public thinking about foreign policy, see John E. Rielly (ed.), *American Public Opinion and U.S. Foreign Policy 1995* (Chicago, Ill.: Chicago Council on Foreign Relations, 1995) and "An Emerging Consensus: A Study of American Public Attitudes on America's Role in the World" (College Park, Md.: Center for International and Security Studies at the University of Maryland, 1996). An even more recent poll (carried on page 2715 of the December 14, 1996, issue of *National Journal*) stated that only 14 percent of Americans wanted the country to be more active in the world, while 40 percent desired that it be less active. Forty-one percent thought the United States should continue its current level of activity.

Chapter 1

The Cold War and Its Demise

How did the age of deregulation come about? Its arrival—along with the end of the Cold War—was neither predictable nor predicted. Still, it is both useful and necessary to retrace this historical transition to appreciate what has changed and what has stayed the same.

The Cold War dominated four and one-half decades of world history, an era like few others in that the competition among the great powers of the day was kept within strict bounds. The contrast with the two previous great-power struggles of the century, both of which culminated in prolonged, destructive conflicts, could not be more marked.

More than anything else, the Cold War derived its "coldness" from the advent of nuclear weapons. The presence of two vast nuclear arsenals and with them the danger of escalation to a nuclear exchange created a mutual interest in avoiding war that dwarfed all other considerations for both the United States and the Soviet Union. Actual war would have meant devastation to the two countries and much of the world so long as both superpowers retained arsenals that could destroy the other's society and economy regardless of which of them struck first. Winston Churchill captured this irony well: "Safety will be the sturdy child of terror, and survival the twin brother of annihilation." For others, it was captured even better by the concept of mutual assured destruction and its acronym, MAD.

It is not enough to point out that both Washington and Moscow went to great lengths to avoid *nuclear* war; what is also true is that leaders of the two superpowers went to great lengths to avoid *any* direct war, lest limited conflict escalate and become unlimited. The result was the emergence of reflexes, understandings, and agreements that bounded competition between the two rivals.

Much of the competition in the military realm involved amassing force that would not be used. Both countries built ever more capable and robust inventories of nuclear weapons. At the same time, the United States and the Soviet Union deployed forces in and around the territory of friends and allies for multiple purposes: to deter attacks, to provide defense if deterrence failed, and, in the case of the USSR, to pressure the West while ensuring the continued existence in Eastern and Central Europe of authoritarian governments loyal to Moscow.

In addition, military competition between the two rivals entailed two other dimensions. First, both superpowers used force to protect clients against external or internal challenge. Thus, the United States intervened directly to defend South Korea after the North invaded and again in South Vietnam against both North Vietnam and the Communists of the South. Second, and on a much smaller scale, the United States deployed force on several occasions within the Western Hemisphere and the Middle East. The Soviet Union periodically intervened (or threatened to) in Eastern Europe—in East Germany and Hungary in the 1950s, Czechoslovakia in the 1960s, Poland in the 1980s—to quell liberal movements. The largest use of force by the USSR, however, contributed to its undoing: the effort begun in 1979 to change and then bolster the government of Afghanistan against rebel forces.

This last point highlights an additional, "indirect" dimension of superpower military competition. Each provided significant military support to friendly governments to help ward off challenges to their authority and to promote security from foes both domestic and foreign. The two also provided support to the respective foes of the other's allies; thus, the United States fought in Vietnam against Soviet-supplied arms while the Soviets had to contend in Afghanistan with antigovernment troops armed in part with U.S.-supplied weapons.[1]

The regulation of U.S.-Soviet relations was less than total. An attempt in 1972 by Henry Kissinger and Richard Nixon to codify ground rules constraining competition—in effect, to enact a de facto concert—failed to make a discernible difference.[2] Neither side was prepared to foreswear seeking unilateral advantage. Indeed, the two approached détente from different perspectives: for the United States, the challenge was how to restrain competition in the context of a competitive relationship, while for the USSR it was how to compete effectively in the context of a restraining relationship.

Still, competition proved to be limited. Rules of the road developed that limited how far either side would go to assist a client against a client of the other. This became most apparent during the October 1973 Middle East conflict, when at various junctures both Washington and Moscow made clear that they would not stand by and see their respective allies—Israel in the case of the United States, Egypt and Syria in the case of the Soviet Union—decimated. There was in addition the acceptance of de facto spheres of influence—Eastern Europe for the USSR, the Americas for the United States—where each placed limits on what it was prepared to do to challenge the position of the other, lest it provoke a crisis that could result in direct confrontation.[3]

There were also more formal agreements in the arms control realm. Several of these placed ceilings on inventories, introducing an important degree of predictability into the entire relationship, even if they did not always lead to reduced military capabilities. There was as well the 1972 limit on ballistic missile defense systems, an agreement that codified stability through mutual vulnerability. There was even limited cooperation in resisting the spread of nuclear weapons capabilities to others, perhaps because the two most powerful states shared an interest in seeing their relative status preserved.[4]

All in all, the Cold War proved to be a highly structured and regulated world. It was dominated by two principal centers of decision making, each heading an alliance or alliances. Any system dominated by two centers of decision making as opposed to a half dozen or more enjoys the inherent advantage of being sturdier and more manageable. It tends to be less dependent on diplomatic acrobatics, in part because there is a smaller number of significant decision makers to contend with.[5] Moreover, the Soviet state was dedicated to controlling national aims in Eastern Europe and within the multinational empire that was the Soviet Union itself. And although the relationships between the United States and both NATO and other allies were much less hierarchical than their East bloc counterparts, Washington did enjoy a degree of influence that gave it considerable leverage.

Also shaping the Cold War world was the fact that the international political and military institutions of the day were dominated by governments—above all, the United States and the Soviet Union. Such institutions enjoyed little autonomy. The United Nations was a victim of the Cold War, more a reflection of its divisions or a locale where they could be played out than anything else. (Soviet support for U.N.-sponsored initiatives against Iraq in 1990–91 underlined the reality that the Cold War had essentially ended.) Economics was the one dimension of international relations that largely excluded the USSR and the rest of the Communist world. In this area, institutions such as the World Bank and the International Monetary Fund were dominated at first by the United States alone and later by wealthy European states, Japan, and the major oil exporters as well.

This highly structured world allowed U.S. foreign policy the luxury of being equally structured. American foreign policy during the Cold War was dominated by containment; in George Kennan's memorable prescription, "the main element of any United States policy toward the Soviet Union must be that of a long-term, patient but vigilant containment of Russian expansive tendencies . . . designed to present the Russians with unalterable counter-force at every point where they show signs of encroaching upon the interests of a peaceful and stable world."[6]

How did the containment doctrine manifest itself in practice? Containment reflected the primacy of the general and global over the particular and local. What mattered most was supporting governments that were anti-Soviet or anti-Communist—or that were at least opposing governments or forces associated with the Soviet Union or communism. What mattered far less was the political and economic nature of the governments the United States supported or even the "rightness" of the details to a local dispute. (One result of these priorities was that many members of the "free world" were anything but free for their citizens.) Containment became a triumph of a narrow realism, of carrying out a foreign policy largely based on the external rather than the internal behavior of governments and other forces.

Within the United States, the policies undertaken early in the Cold War pursuant to containment (and the funding of tools to promote them) were widely supported by Republicans and Democrats alike. Congress routinely acquiesced to presidential leadership, in large part because many believed that in time of war (the Cold War being a form of permanent war) it was right to rally behind the commander in chief. There was also a willingness to defer to the executive branch on the grounds that it was better informed. And even where congressional acquiescence was missing, the president was still able to dominate foreign policymaking because of the relative weakness of levers available to Congress and, under the Constitution, the unique ability of the executive to take initiative overseas. Only the president can send troops abroad, negotiate treaties and other pacts, and speak in the name of the American people to peoples and governments of other lands.

Consensus over foreign policy—never complete to begin with—unraveled in earnest in the late 1960s. Vietnam was the most salient cause, as a significant minority (if not a majority) of the country and Congress came to the conclusion that U.S. interests at stake in Vietnam did not justify the investment and/or that U.S. policy was flawed in design, execution, or both. Doubts created by Vietnam were reinforced by Watergate. At issue was not simply where and how to apply containment but the desirability of executive leadership in the application.

Despite important exceptions, including the decisions to resist Soviet intervention in Afghanistan and match the Soviet military buildup, agreement over the goals and conduct of U.S. foreign policy eroded further over the next 15 years, i.e., from 1975 to 1990, during the post-Vietnam period. This evolution in attitudes reflected the residue of the bitter divisions over Vietnam and a waning of the Cold War's intensity. Major debates raged over how to respond to the conflict in El Salvador and the emergence of a Soviet-supported regime in Nicaragua, over whether to counter the deployment of a new generation of intermediate-range Soviet missiles in Europe, and over the emphasis that ought to be accorded human rights concerns in Communist and friendly non-Communist countries alike. It was also a period of growing tension between the two branches of government as Congress asserted new powers through legislation and new capacities through the expansion of staff. What had been for some an imperial presidency became for others imperiled.[7]

Demographic changes within the United States also had a corrosive effect upon the old foreign policy consensus. In the post–World War II era, U.S. foreign policy was dominated by an elite that was for the most part highly educated, internationally and especially European-oriented, and based in the Northeast. This generation took from history the lesson that the greatest threat to world peace was American isolation. American effort and leadership, something best represented by victory in World War II, became a model of international engagement.

A half-century later, the country's population had grown to over 260 million, up from 140 million. Americans of European descent no longer dominated. Population shifted away from the Northeast toward the Sunbelt, where people often were more interested in developments to their south or in Asia and the Pacific rather than across the Atlantic. Together, these developments tended to dilute the intensity of ties to Europe. In addition, by the mid-1990s, most of those Americans whose world views had been forged by events early this century had either retired or died. Korea and more often Vietnam were the defining international experiences for younger generations. If Korea left many Americans frustrated, Vietnam left even more questioning the morality of U.S. leadership and the utility of military force—to the extent that international developments left any impression on them at all.

The intellectual debate also changed. In the wake of World War II, there were few institutions and few publications devoted to international affairs. The Council on Foreign Relations and its quarterly *Foreign Affairs* were dominant. Three networks and a handful of newspapers shaped elite opinion. Within a few decades, think tanks, publications, and channels all had proliferated, representing diverse views and styles of presentation, thereby further dividing what had been a largely cohesive foreign policy establishment.

The final reason for the breakdown of consensus over foreign policy—certainly the proverbial straw that broke the camel's back—was its success. Containment was no longer relevant with the Soviet threat not only contained but eliminated. Suddenly it became much more important to discuss the inherent importance of interests rather than simply respond to challenges to counter or preempt a global competitor. And without a clear and overriding threat or ideological adversary, it became more difficult to justify the expenditure of resources on behalf of national security. The traditional "guns-versus-butter" debate shifted in favor of the latter, given the reduction in external threats to the country's well-being and the corresponding increase in threats to economic and social welfare from within.

What led to the West's victory in the Cold War is worth contemplating. In part it was fundamental Soviet weakness, the result of the USSR's being top-heavy, overcentralized both politically and economically. Here it is possible to cite a long list of consequences, including an unproductive economic system, corruption, the pull of nationalism and the failed attempts to repress ethnicity and religion, political alienation and the collapse of communist ideology, the absence of a mechanism for orderly succession, and persistent poor leadership.[8]

The USSR was a victim as well of what the historian Paul Kennedy termed "imperial overstretch," the tendency of great powers to undermine the economic sources of their greatness by devoting too much of their wealth and energies to overseas adventures rather than to investments that would allow them to maintain their competitive position.[9] The Soviet Union was a classic case of a country that devoted scarce resources to overseas ventures while it starved its own society. It could have had its cake and eaten it, but only if it had reduced its allocation of resources to defense, been less eager to support far-flung expansionist enterprises, and, more important, undertaken economic reforms that would have reduced the size and role of the state. It is difficult to find fault with Henry Kissinger's assessment that "the Soviet Union was neither strong enough nor dynamic enough for the role its leaders had assigned it."[10]

But the Soviet Union lasted 75 years. It was by no means inevitable that it would collapse—and certainly not when it did. Mikhail Gorbachev clearly hastened the end. His principal reforms—*perestroika* and *glasnost*—weakened central authority and increased the power of the media and civil society at the expense of the existing order. Gorbachev could have held the country together longer, but only if he was willing to be as repressive as some of his predecessors, something he clearly rejected. The weakening of central control, and the reluctance to act brutally to reassert such control, doomed a system (and a state) that required repression to exist.[11]

But American and, more broadly, Western strength also contributed significantly to the breakup of the Soviet empire. Both what the United States *was* and what it *did* had an impact. By what the United States "was" I mean the example of and the impression made by American society. The clear success of capitalism and the vitality of American democracy put a lie to Soviet predictions of victory and made the Soviet Union look poor and gray by comparison, which it was. This perception led to a loss of faith in Communist ideology and widespread public cynicism throughout the USSR.

American and other Western efforts in the defense realm also certainly helped persuade the Soviet Union not to use force. The result was to neutralize the one dimension of power in which the Soviet Union was truly super and to place the competition in realms in which the United States and the West enjoyed marked advantages. As the English historian Michael Howard pointed out, "The Cold War was won by the triumph of the global market economies over the Marxist-Leninist command economies—or, if you prefer, pluralist democracy over totalitarianism. But this triumph was made possible only by the stable framework provided by military deterrence."[12] Thomas Powers makes a related point: "Time is what containment took and time is what the fear of nuclear war gave us."[13]

A number of specific decisions in the defense realm—the Berlin airlift, decades of NATO modernization and expansion, the willingness to deploy cruise and intermediate-range ballistic missiles in the 1980s in response to the presence of Soviet SS-20 missiles, the arming of the Afghan resistance, a heightened emphasis on ballistic missile defense—also hastened the end of the Cold War. These and other Western actions denied the Soviet Union any sense of momentum. It thus became impossible for even the most committed Communist to argue with any degree of credibility that history was moving in the USSR's favor.

The advent of détente—the mellowing of the U.S.-Soviet relationship as compared with both the Cold War and peaceful coexistence—denied the USSR an enemy. In the process, it became harder to justify the political repression and permanent war footing at home. Détente also helped open up the Soviet Union and the Eastern bloc to visitors and ideas, thereby undermining the official monopoly over information. Last but far from least was the cumulative effect of decades of military buildup and the extension of military and economic assistance to friends, allies, and proxies—competitions much more easily sustained by the more productive economies of the West. In short, the Cold War was not simply lost by one side, it was won by the other.[14] The lesson is clear: what the United States does and does not do can help determine history.[15]

The result of all these changes and the Cold War's end is a very different United States that has to contend with a very different world. As Kenneth Waltz noted, "Wars that eliminate enough rival great powers are system-transforming wars."[16] The Cold War's elimination of the Soviet Union certainly qualifies; while multipolarity can in principle survive the loss of one of its protagonists, bipolarity cannot. It would be strange indeed if the policies and institutions that for the most part served this country well for the Cold War were able to do the same in the world that is taking its place.

NOTES

1. Peter W. Rodman, *More Precious than Peace: The Cold War and the Struggle for the Third World* (New York: Scribner's, 1994).
2. "Basic Principles of Relations Between the United States of America and the Union of Soviet Socialist Republics," in *Public Papers of the Presidents of the United States: Richard Nixon 1972* (Washington, D.C.: U.S. Government Printing Office, 1974), 633–35.
3. On this and related points accounting for Cold War stability, see John Lewis Gaddis, *The Long Peace: Inquiries into the History of the Cold War* (New York: Oxford University Press, 1987), especially 215–45.
4. See Albert Carnesale and Richard N. Haass (eds.), *Superpower Arms Control: Setting the Record Straight* (Cambridge, Mass.: Ballinger, 1987).
5. See, for example, Kenneth N. Waltz, *Theory of International Politics* (Reading, Mass.: Addison-Wesley, 1979), 161–63.
6. See George F. Kennan, "The Sources of Soviet Conduct," in his *American Diplomacy 1900–1950* (Chicago: University of Chicago Press, 1951), 99, 104. For background, see John Lewis Gaddis, *Strategies of Containment* (New York: Oxford University Press, 1982).
7. There is a large literature on the relative rise of Congress in the realm of foreign and defense policy. See my *Congress and American Security Policy* (London: International Institute for Strategic Studies, 1978).
8. See, for example, the articles in the Spring 1993 issue (Number 31) of *National Interest*; Richard J. Barnet, "A Balance Sheet: Lippmann, Kennan and the End of the Cold War," in Michael J. Hogan (ed.), *The End of the Cold War: Its Meaning and Implications* (Cambridge: Cambridge University Press, 1992), especially 116; and Robert W. Tucker, "1989 and All That," in Nicholas X. Rizopoulos (ed.), *Sea-Changes: American Foreign Policy in a World Transformed* (New York: Council on Foreign Relations, 1990), 204–37.
9. Paul Kennedy, *The Rise and Fall of the Great Powers: Economic Change and Military Conflict from 1500 to 2000* (New York: Random House, 1987).
10. Henry Kissinger, *Diplomacy* (New York: Simon & Schuster, 1994), 764.
11. See John Lewis Gaddis, *The United States and the End of the Cold War* (New York: Oxford University Press, 1992), especially 156–62.
12. Michael Howard, "Lessons of the Cold War," *Survival* 36, no. 4 (Winter 1994–95), 166.
13. Thomas Powers, "Who Won the Cold War?" *New York Review of Books* 43, no. 8 (June 20, 1996), 27.
14. Jack Matlock, the former U.S. ambassador to the Soviet Union, makes a useful distinction among the end of the Cold War, the end of Soviet communism, and the end of the Soviet Union. He accords the United States and the West the critical role in ending the Cold War. Gorbachev is cited as being the person most responsible for the end of Soviet communism, and former KGB chairman Vladimir Kryuchkov (among others) for the demise of the union itself. See Jack F. Matlock Jr., *Autopsy on an Empire: The American Ambas-*

sador's Account of the Collapse of the Soviet Union (New York: Random House, 1995), especially 667–72.

15. For those who desire more of this debate, three books suggest the available range of views. See Robert M. Gates, *From the Shadows: The Ultimate Insider's Story of Five Presidents and How They Won the Cold War* (New York: Simon & Schuster, 1996); Raymond L. Garthoff, *The Great Transition: American-Soviet Relations and the End of the Cold War* (Washington, D.C.: Brookings, 1994); and Jay Winik, *On the Brink: The Dramatic, Behind-the-Scenes Saga of the Reagan Era and the Men and Women Who Won the Cold War* (New York: Simon & Schuster, 1996). Garthoff attributes the end of the Cold War mostly to Gorbachev and the USSR. Winik emphasizes American (especially Reagan-era) policies. Gates comes out somewhere in between, with the added wrinkle of seeing Reagan less as a departure than someone who continued Carter's more aggressive approach. Also, see Thomas Risse-Kappen, "Did 'Peace Through Strength' End the Cold War? Lessons from INF," *International Security* 16, no. 1 (Summer 1991), 162–88, and Richard Pipes, "Misinterpreting the Cold War: The Hard-Liners Had It Right," *Foreign Affairs* 74, no. 1 (January–February 1995), 154–60. Pipes's position is obvious from his title. Risse-Kappen argues just the opposite, that domestic politics within the USSR and not Western strength was critical. Clearly, both factors were at work and, like most debates, this one is over degree.

16. Waltz, *Theory of International Politics* (Reading, Mass.: Addison-Wesley, 1979), 199.

Chapter 2

The Age of Deregulation

A sure sign that experts are encountering difficulty with figuring something out is their use of "post–" as a prefix. Such a label reveals that people know only where they have been, not where they are now, much less where they are heading.

The post–Cold War world is one such period of uncertainty. We have been in this situation for the better part of a decade. Being more specific than that is difficult. It is possible to date V-E or V-J Day with precision, but V-CW Day is elusive. For some it was November 1989, when the Berlin Wall was first breached. For others, the end of the Cold War did not arrive until more than two years later, when the Russian Tricolor was raised over the Kremlin, signifying the end of the Soviet experiment. Alternative signposts for when the Cold War ended, including German unification or U.S.-Soviet cooperation during the Gulf crisis, are no less plausible. But even if we could agree, it would not solve the immediate problem of what to call the present.

One way to come up with a title is to hold a contest. The *New York Times* did this not long ago; I have been unable to locate the results but confess to a bit of skepticism all the same.[1] A more tested approach is to wait. Time often clears things up. This, after all, is the principal advantage historians have over journalists.

Thus, the Dark Ages were deemed to lack light only in retrospect; by definition, the Middle Ages could not have been named at the time. In the end, it took nothing less than the Renaissance.

For better or worse, those alive now lack the luxury of waiting for history to sort itself out. The only real choice is to begin to make sense of the present. It is essential that we do so, for only by understanding what exists can we even hope to fashion and carry out a foreign policy for bringing about what we want. It will not be easy. A substantial part of what was thought or written about international relations and American foreign policy since World War II no longer applies. The end of the Cold War, the demise of the construct of loose bipolarity that dominated U.S.-Soviet relations and world politics, is the political equivalent of some stunning scientific breakthrough—for example, when Copernicus persuaded people that Ptolemy was wrong that the earth revolved around the sun and not vice versa—that makes obsolete a good deal of what was previously taken as a given.

There is an important distinction between the physical and the social sciences, however. In the former, what changes is our understanding of the world rather than the world itself. To return to Copernicus, it was not that the heavens had altered their orbits, only mankind's ability to comprehend what had long existed. But with the end of the Cold War, the world itself has changed, necessitating a revision in our understanding. This may make it easier to let go of the old construct, but it remains no less difficult to identify a new model to take its place. As James Rosenau noted, "To recognize the rapidity with which a paradigm crumbles when it starts to go is not to discern the outlines and basic premises of those that might evolve in its place. A long period of disarray and tension may have to ensue before the essential components of a new paradigm are pieced together into a structured and parsimonious whole."[2]

VISION THINGS

A number of visions or paradigms have been proposed for what the post–Cold War era is or is becoming. One of the first to be articulated is also one of the most optimistic: Francis Fukuyama's "End of History." Fukuyama argues on behalf of a liberal, democratic paradigm that the end of the Cold War era was made possible by the triumph of liberal political and economic ideas over their Communist and statist rivals. The result of this triumph is not only more prosperous and free societies but a world in which relations among states are likely to be harmonious.[3]

Subsequent world views were noticeably darker. The first, put forward by John Mearsheimer, suggested that a Europe no longer divided by two nuclear superpowers of roughly equal military strength might be prone to violence caused by "hypernationalism." Alas, Mearsheimer's predictions in this realm proved to be all too accurate, even if his expectation of great-power rivalry has not come to pass and his recommendations (which included propping up the Soviet Union and encouraging a German nuclear capability) were of questionable wisdom.[4]

Two other pessimistic perspectives, seemingly influenced by intervening events in Africa and the former Yugoslavia, also stand out: Robert Kaplan's "The Coming Anarchy" and Samuel Huntington's "The Clash of Civilizations?" Both offer far darker images of the future. Where they differ is in their scale. Kaplan sees a world in which nation-states break down into small, often dysfunctional pieces. His is a world of multiple Somalias, Rwandas, Haitis, Liberias, and Bosnias, a world in which governments are often at the mercy of drug cartels, criminal organizations, and terrorists. A modern-day Conrad, Kaplan looks at the evolving post–Cold War world and sees Africa at its worst writ large.[5]

Huntington sees the world divided into far larger pieces, defined by civilizations, notably Western, Sinic, Japanese, Islamic, Hindu, Slavic-Orthodox, Latin American, and African. "People and countries with similar cultures are coming together. People and countries with different cultures are coming apart. . . . Cultural communities are replacing Cold War blocs, and the fault lines between civilizations are becoming the central lines of conflict in global politics."[6] Some civilizations correspond to existing nation–states while others include several or parts of several. It is a world of tension and potential violence, but on a much higher level.

In Huntington's view, clashes between civilizations are likely to increase over time, owing to fundamental differences on how civic and social life ought to be ordered and the fact that different civilizations cannot avoid one another in an increasingly interdependent world. Huntington also cites the weakening of political ties so that civilizational identities and associations fill a gap, a negative reaction in large parts of the world to the existing primacy of the West and the United States in particular, and the growth of economic regionalism that is both a cause and a reflection of civilizational allegiances.

Two other perspectives focus more on the balance of power. One of these (popularized by Charles Krauthammer) sees the post–Cold War world as essentially unipolar, in which the vacuum left by the Soviet Union's demise has come to be filled by the United States rather than by a collection of others or by chaos.[7] The second perspective sees the post–Cold War world more as a multipolar balance of power that is relatively stable. In this view, bipolarity has given way to either a balanced multipolarity or to a system akin to a "concert" in which the principal members not only balance one another but agree on many of the rules and norms governing international life.[8]

Still others have put forward images that focus more on structural changes. One popular theory is the decline of the nation-state, the basic unit of account of international relations for the past three centuries. One of the principal proponents of this view, Kenichi Omae, argues that economic ties will transcend national borders, resulting in new "natural economic zones" or "regional states" that will become the groupings that matter the most.[9] And there is a view that could hardly be more different, namely, that despite the end of the Cold War, little has changed. In this case, the author (G. John Ikenberry) argues that the pre–Cold War order created in the middle and late 1940s and characterized by the Atlantic Charter, international trade and financial institutions, and the United Nations, has not only survived but prevailed.[10]

Several individuals, including Benjamin Barber and John Lewis Gaddis, have noted the simultaneous and in some ways contradictory trends of globalization and disintegration—or integration and fragmentation.[11] To them, the world is both coming together and apart at the same time. A related concept is that of unevenness, in which large areas of the world are characterized by peace, democracy, and economic prosperity at the same time that other areas are experiencing political turmoil, conflict, and poverty.[12] In this view, the post–Cold War world is less a single entity that permits generalization than the sum of its different and distinct elements.

These last two perspectives come closest to reflecting the emerging reality. It certainly is preferable to the more one-dimensional visions. The positive vision of a world of liberal democracies living in harmony simply does not comport with a reality that is often anything but harmonious and in which many societies are and will remain less than completely democratic. Meanwhile, the Kaplan vision of disintegration ignores the many examples of globalization and progress, just as the Huntington future of cultural conflict fails to account adequately for the power of states and forces such as nationalism that are often dominant and can lead to associations that cross religious and cultural lines.[13]

The personality of the post–Cold War world is captured most accurately and comprehensively by the concept of "international deregulation." We have moved from a highly structured world dominated by two or at most a few to a less structured world of the many. New technologies have emerged and spread, in the process transforming political, economic, and military relationships. The effects of the change are anything but uniform; not all citizens or states have felt the same political or economic impact. New rules, relationships, and arrangements have yet to evolve to harness all this dynamism and maintain order. The result is a world that may well be safer, in that the chances of cataclysmic conflict are arguably less, but also a world that is less stable, where smaller but still highly destructive conflicts within, between, and among states are more common than before.

The phrase "international deregulation" is consciously derived from the world of economics and government. The closest parallel is to the aviation industry in the United States. It was just two decades ago that the airline industry was among this country's most structured. There were a limited number of major carriers—

Pan American, Eastern, Delta, United, American, Braniff, TWA—and a few smaller regional lines. Little changed in the industry from year to year. The same cities were served. Prices were fairly predictable and often differed only modestly among airlines if at all.

Twenty years of airline deregulation has spawned a very different industry. Although the number of airlines has increased significantly, some of the principal carriers of the past are gone. Still others have combined into enormous companies. Airlines today fly more flights, carry more passengers, and employ more workers. Revenues are up but profits are not. Although ticket prices have declined overall, they have become much more volatile. Few passengers on the same plane are likely to be paying the same price—and prices bear little correlation to the distance between points. The average time for a flight has increased, the result of air and ground congestion. The development of regional "hubs and spokes" has increased the need for passengers to change planes, although such changes are far more likely than before to be within rather than between carriers. Planes are more crowded; so, too, are airports. New airports have been built, as have new models of aircraft. Some cities have lost some or all of their service; others enjoy more than before. And safety has improved, despite the widespread perception that deregulation has had the opposite result. In short, deregulation has unleashed a multitude of effects, some of them desirable, others clearly unwelcome.[14]

This is not to suggest that the parallel between the worlds of post–Cold War international relations and domestic aviation is exact. Most obviously, post–Cold War deregulation is a development, not the product of conscious design. Nor does the concept of deregulation capture every element of emerging international life. But we should keep in mind that the Cold War paradigm did not reflect every aspect of the previous era of international relations. But this is not the point. As Thomas Kuhn has pointed out, "To be accepted as a paradigm, a theory must seem better than its competitors, but it need not, and in fact never does, explain all the facts with which it can be confronted."[15] In this, the bipolar Cold War paradigm qualified. So, now, does deregulation.

What are the principal features of a deregulated world? Three stand out. The first involves a loosening of international relations—the emergence of new centers of decision making, a corresponding diffusion of power, and an absence of universally accepted norms. Second, the nation-state is weaker, having lost some of its authority to new actors on the international scene at the same time it has become increasingly vulnerable to forces that respect no border. Third, a majority of the world lives, for the moment, in societies that are mostly democratic and market-oriented, a change that reflects the widespread appeal of these models and the perceived failure of the Soviet model of state control over political and economic life. Together, these three trends make for a world that is fundamentally different from the world of the Cold War.

GLOBAL LOOSENING

It is unlikely that during the Cold War, Iraq would have been left free by the Soviet Union, a principal source of its arms, to invade a country in a region known to be of vital interest to the West. (The invasion by North Korea of the South some 40 years before can in part be explained by real doubt as to whether the West would come to South Korea's aid.) Similarly, it is far from certain that either China or Russia has the ability today to persuade North Korea to forgo the development of nuclear weapons, something that could set it on a collision course with the United States. And the most terrible of post–Cold War crises, in the former Yugoslavia, was made possible by the demise of authoritarian rule in Moscow and Belgrade and in the subsequent loss of control over local events.

The centrifugal effect of loosening is partially offset by the greater ease of using military force or conducting diplomacy by the United States without fear of engaging a rival superpower. On balance, though, decentralized decision making and the diffusion of political authority increases the potential for international challenges and crises, even if it also decreases their international significance. Some will disagree, arguing that the world is more orderly after the Cold War, the result of no more Soviet mischief-making and greater American dominance. But as we have seen, there were limits to the Soviet propensity for risk. More important, American "dominance" is anything but total. Yes, the United States emerged from the Cold War as the world's most powerful state. And, yes, Bosnia makes clear that the United States can still make a crucial difference—by what it does and what it chooses not to do. (Anyone doubting this need only contemplate the gap between what the West accomplished prior to mid-1995 and subsequently, thanks in large part to the liberal use of airpower and the forceful diplomacy of Richard Holbrooke.) Moreover, Bosnia was by no means unique. The Gulf War coalition, the creation of the World Trade Organization, the financial rescue of the Mexican government, the change of government in Haiti, the denucleariza-tion of Ukraine and two other states once part of the USSR—these and other cases attest to the unique capacity of the United States to effect change in the post–Cold War world.

But primacy is not to be confused with hegemony. The United States cannot compel others to become more democratic. Nor can it intervene with military force everywhere or dictate that another government join in sanctioning a third country in situations where there is no common perception of the threat or agreement on how best to meet it. Here, too, there are examples. U.S. attempts to isolate Iran, Libya, Vietnam, and Cuba have failed to varying degrees. The United States has been unable to halt Chinese exports of nuclear materials or compel Chinese respect of human rights, persuade Syria to make peace with Israel, lead Japan to fully open its markets, convince Egypt to liberalize politically, or stop Russian military offensives against Chechnya. The list goes on. The point is that influence is necessarily finite as a result of limits to American resources and the capacity of others to resist.

More important, U.S. primacy is not simply limited—the United States in the wake of the Cold War is less dominant in world affairs than it was after World War II, although even then it was far from all-powerful—but it is, on balance, eroding. It is noteworthy that Charles Krauthammer titled his provocative article "The Unipolar Moment."[16] A moving picture rather than a snapshot would depict the reality that the U.S. share of the world's wealth is falling, even though U.S. output is rising in absolute terms. Similarly, and although the United States leads in virtually any measure of military might, conventional or unconventional, it cannot be assured that it will enjoy local superiority in many situations. Politically, the United States cannot demand and obtain agreement in the U.N. Security Council or in NATO. No one state can insist on others adopting its preferred definition of what constitutes desirable behavior vis-à-vis its neighbors and its own citizens. Aaron Friedberg captures this situation well: "The diffusion of power . . . is likely to result not in a single, epic convulsion, followed by a rapid consolidation of a new order, but rather in a period of many simultaneous, lower-level disputes over existing institutions and practices. This interval of declining legitimacy and increasing instability is already well under way, and given the nature of the changes that underlie it, there is reason to expect that it will persist for some time."[17]

Another sign that primacy is eroding is that allies are less certain to follow or provide support. It is terribly difficult to enlist participation in some military endeavor or sanction, especially if the challenge involves interests or threats that fall outside the original mission or area of the alliance. (The Gulf War was an exception, in large part because of the presence of oil, Saddam's blatant aggression, and the determination of the Bush administration to act.) That this is increasingly the case should come as no surprise; alliances are most often formed and animated by what members oppose, and the demise of the Soviet Union left most formal groupings without a clear raison d'être.

In a related development, it is possible to discern and anticipate a revival of what might be called traditional great-power politics. The world may not divide anymore along an East-West axis, but powerful states in several regions have the ability to challenge the United States. Traditional friends and allies (France being an obvious one) have demonstrated a greater willingness to stake out positions supportive of narrow national interests. Relationships among friends as a rule are becoming more complex and "situational" rather than consistent. More important, former adversaries are anything but assured partners. Russia and China have demonstrated a willingness and ability to conduct policies that run contrary to U.S. efforts and objectives. While these countries no longer reflexively take an opposing view to U.S. positions, they still are engaged in power politics, pursuing their national interests as shaped by history, geography, culture, economics, and domestic affairs.

These and related changes are especially noticeable in the Asia-Pacific region, increasingly the locus of the world's greatest concentration of wealth. Moreover, projections are that the region's share of global output will grow not only in absolute terms but relative to the rest of the world. In 1995, for example, U.S. gross domestic product nearly equaled that of Japan, China, Indonesia, South Korea, and Thailand combined. In 25 years, it is estimated that U.S. output (which will double during that time) will be less than 40 percent that of these same countries.[18]

Such an increase in wealth is of obvious economic significance to the United States. The region's markets will be a critical outlet for U.S. exports and investment; the region's goods, capital, and technology will be important for the U.S. market and economy. But the growing importance of the region transcends just the economic. History strongly suggests that rising economic power translates into increased military and political power.[19] This translation is already taking effect, as a pronounced buildup of modern conventional armaments is already underway in China, Taiwan, Japan, the Republic of Korea, and the ASEAN states. The old order in the Asia-Pacific region, based on American primacy and allegiances born of the Cold War, is giving way to a new configuration in which China and Japan and possibly others will become more central while other local states increasingly look to themselves or to their neighbors for their security.

Such change could well trigger conflict. As Robert Gilpin has noted, "the most destabilizing factor is the tendency in an international system for the powers of member states to change at different rates because of political, economic and technological developments. In time, the differential growth in power of the various states in the system causes a fundamental redistribution of power in the system."[20] The challenge will come in managing the transition to this new situation and in the outcome itself, that is, in working to see that any new "balance" is in fact "balanced" from our perspective. This will prove especially difficult in the Asia-Pacific area, given the large number of major powers (China, Japan, Russia, and the United States), the even larger number of medium-sized powers (the two Koreas, Taiwan, the Association of Southeast Asian [ASEAN] states of Indonesia, Thailand, Singapore, Malaysia, Philippines, and Brunei), and the region's many unre-solved disputes, including the Korean peninsula (where prolonged economic decline could cause the North to collapse), Taiwan, and the Spratley Islands in addition to a number of long-standing bor-der disagreements.[21] The fact that this part of the world for the most part lacks regional institutions (especially in the political and military realms) only adds to the uncertainty; indeed, the contrast with what exists in Europe could hardly be more pronounced.

Also altering the balance of power around the globe is the proliferation of military power. The spread of advanced conven-tional and unconventional military technologies—chemical, bio-logical, and nuclear materials, as well as the ballistic missiles to deliver them—is already extensive and promises to become much more so.[22] A recent publication by the U.S. intelligence commu-nity judged that at least 20 countries, nearly half in the Middle East, Persian Gulf, and South Asia, already have or may be devel-oping weapons of mass destruction and ballistic missile delivery systems.[23]

The phenomenon of unconventional weapons proliferation has the clear potential to grow worse. One of the direct conse-quences of the breakup of the Soviet Union and subsequent politi-cal and economic instability is the dilution of control over nuclear weapons and fissile materials. At issue are literally tens of thou-sands of nuclear weapons and enough material to make several tens of thousands more. The greatest danger is that some of this material could fall into the hands of some terrorist group or rogue state, thereby providing it the means to fashion a crude but still deadly nuclear device.[24]

All proliferation risks bringing about new instabilities. Those who possess unconventional weapons may be tempted to use them. Those who do not possess them, or those who see themselves as especially vulnerable to unconventional warfare, may be tempted to act against these capabilities before they can be fully deployed or employed by adversaries. And there is a greater potential for devastation if order breaks down.[25]

Not everyone agrees. One school of thought holds that proliferation of weapons of mass destruction can enhance stability by introducing the same sort of caution and rules of the road that characterized the U.S.-Soviet relationship.[26] Indeed, proliferation may have had just this impact in South Asia, where there are signs that India and Pakistan are managing their relationship with greater care now that both possess nuclear weapons capabilities. It was this same logic that led one analyst to argue for Ukraine's holding on to its nuclear weapons and for Germany to acquire them.[27]

Still, such thinking is controversial for good reason. Should a conflict involve unconventional weapons, the consequences would be as awful as they were great. In most instances, proliferation promises to bring more problems than it solves by increasing the temptation of preventive and preemptive attacks, especially as much of the proliferation that we see is taking place in regions with a history of conflict. States with less than robust capabilities, i.e, those that cannot survive a strike by an opponent, invite attack before such weapons are employed. Surviving the transition from emerging to robust or mature arsenals capable of deterrence is likely to prove extremely difficult. Political and physical control over nuclear weapons cannot be assured in countries with powerful independent militaries or strong separatist movements, or where terrorist and criminal organizations exist unchecked. The result is that while proliferation may turn out to enhance stability in selected situations, in most it will have just the opposite effect.

The diffusion of military power reinforces trends toward deregulation in another way. It will make it more difficult for the United States and others to use force effectively. Many of the would-be proliferators—Iran, Iraq, Libya, North Korea—are rogue states and potential battlefield antagonists of the United States. Desert Storm may have made matters worse; one of its perverse consequences was to increase the appeal of weapons of mass destruction as an "equalizer" capable of offsetting U.S. advantages in advanced conventional munitions. At a minimum, the proliferation of weapons of mass destruction will raise the human and financial costs of intervention, thereby narrowing the options for the number of military undertakings that might be carried out at any one time or within a given period.

STATE OF CHANGE

The increasing number of actors on the international scene and the *relative* decline in the centrality of the nation-state is a second critical development. For hundreds of years, states have been the basic unit of international relations. Now, one encounters books with the title *The End of the Nation State* or declarations that "By many measures, corporations are today more central players in global affairs than nations."[28] An influential journal recently published an entire issue under the title "What Future for the State?"[29] The fact that it is deemed necessary even to ask suggests a future for the traditional state that is considerably less than bright.

It is correct that most of the new actors (or actors that are familiar in name but much enhanced in capacity) are not nation-states at all. Some of these actors complement what states do; some challenge or even threaten states. There are those that constrain or affect the state from "above," including global institutions (the United Nations, the International Monetary Fund, the World Bank, the World Trade Organization) or regional organizations (NATO, the European Union, ASEAN, etc.). Other entities buffet the state from "below" or from the "side." A short list of those in this category include nongovernmental organizations (Amnesty International, Greenpeace, Doctors Without Borders), criminal gangs, drug cartels, ethnic groups seeking independence, terrorist groups, media, religious orders, and multinational corporations.[30]

The are several reasons for the explosion in nonstate actors. Many of those groups acting from "below" or alongside the state level seek to fill a perceived void, to carry out functions or promote agendas not met by states. Fundamentally different are those groups that are enemies of states, that carry out illegal activity. Their goal is not to complement the limitations of states but to exploit them. In the case of developments above the state level, such as regional or international organizations, states themselves have created or encouraged the activism of these entities in recognition that association with such bodies is in their self-interest. In still other instances, such as multinational corporations, states tend to see the value of independent agents and make it possible for them to act.

Why is any of this necessarily deregulating? To some extent it is a function of numbers; it is always more difficult to coordinate numerous entities than a few. But it is also because of both the strength and the weakness of most of these nonstate actors. Quite a few of them have very different notions of what is desirable in the world and how to bring it about. They also increasingly have the capacity to promote their own agendas, be it by producing or purchasing arms, by circumventing sanctions, by controlling information, or amassing wealth. At the same time, none of these nonstate entities is capable of acting like a great power and regulating the world on its own. International organizations in particular tend to be constrained by the need for consensus among members—who happen to be states.

For this and other reasons, it is important not to dismiss the state as obsolete or irrelevant. What is relevant is not simply the existence of such groups (and their growing number) but their influence. A good deal of what Ethan Kapstein describes as "home country control" remains.[31] Governments retain the ability to restrict (if not control) access, be it to manufactured goods, services, drugs, or people. They can cooperate to slow the spread of selected technologies to certain would-be recipients. Governments can set policies—for example, by what they do in the realm of fiscal and monetary policy or in investment codes—that influence the behavior of nonstate actors. States can prevent action by any global or regional organization that requires consensus or where jurisdiction must be accepted as a prerequisite for action. They can abridge or enhance the political and human rights of their people. Most important, states are by far the greatest holders of military power.[32]

The result, again, is a deregulated world that is neither fully regulated nor anarchic. Individual states, while continuing to be the most powerful units in the world, do not enjoy anything resembling a monopoly or even near-monopoly of power or control. There are many more centers of decision making, far more actors on the world stage responsible only or mostly to themselves and their own agendas. It is much more difficult for any single actor to impose its will or preferences. International organizations have more authority in many cases than before, but still far from enough to deter or resolve most forms of conflict. The bipolarity of the Cold War has given way not simply to multipolarity but to a complex form of it in which states and nonstates interact in a host of contexts and situations.

Reinforcing the trend toward the relative weakening of the nation-state is the globalization of economic relations. A number of developments are captured by this concept, including the expanded volume of world trade and its greater importance to participants, increased flows of private investment capital, and reliance on external sources of raw materials. There is as well the progress in trade liberalization through such arrangements as the North American Free Trade Area (NAFTA), Latin America's Mercusor, the European Union (EU), the Asia-Pacific's APEC, and the World Trade Organization (WTO)—and a simultaneous jump in trade disputes and demands for protectionist policies. There is also the growing privatization of global economics, signaled by the peso crisis of December 1994, which showed the power of mutual fund managers, just as the decision of a company headquartered halfway around the world on whether to build a manufacturing plant in a particular country can determine whether thousands there get a regular paycheck. The relative value of a nation's currency is something that governments and central banks can only influence, not control.

The consequences of these multiple factors are several and far from simple. On the one hand, growing economic interdependence is a regulating phenomenon, in that more parties have more of a stake in maintaining the relatively open flow of manufactured goods, technology, raw materials, services, and capital. Also, there are new mechanisms for the resolution of economic disputes. On the other hand, economic globalization is deregulating, as the ability of the United States or any other government to control its economic fate is reduced by the decisions of foreign firms, governments, international institutions, and investors. Interdependence is also deregulating because it makes it impossible to escape from frictions or conflicts caused by the reality of dependence.

Making economic globalization possible but also a factor in its own right is the globalization of information. Governments of all sorts are weaker in the face of new technologies that respect no border and that empower individuals, groups, and corporations. McLuhan was right. The corollary is that Orwell and his image of a future in which technology strengthened the organs of the state and its capacity to control its citizenry could not have been more wrong. The world of the Cold War—essentially, the world between 1950 and 1990—was one in which governments dominated their societies. Computers were rare and large; only toward the end of the era were they sufficiently small and affordable so that individuals could have access to them (not to mention communicate with one another through them). For much of the Cold War fax technology did not exist. International telephone calls required operators. Television was almost entirely national and, with the exception of the United States, tended to be controlled by governments which allowed only a few channels.

Information and communications technology have come to serve the individual more than the state. Few states can win the fight against laptop computers, international direct dialing, fax machines, satellite dishes, the Internet, and modems.[33] As Jessica Mathews has noted, "Widely accessible and affordable technology has broken governments' monopoly on the collection and management of large amounts of information and deprived governments of the deference they enjoyed because of it."[34] Even the United States, for all its sophistication, is vulnerable both to the impact of images and to the effects of their absence, i.e., issues tend to lose some or all of their salience when journalists cannot report on them or cameras reach them. This helps explain why some human rights atrocities have less impact on the international community than others.

How does this contribute to deregulation? Technology increases the scope and impact of communications across state borders, making it much more difficult for governments to control what their citizens know and what others know about them. It increases pressures on governments to act (and gives them less time to decide) while it simultaneously constrains them. This was, for example, the contradictory effect of the media on the U.S. military intervention in Somalia, which was both stimulated by images of suffering and then undermined by images of a dead American soldier being dragged through the streets. Regulation is about management, and increasingly technology is something that resists it.

States are also feeling the effect of the changing character of nationalism. With the relaxation of external threats and alliance systems and the erosion of both empires and multinational states, nationalism has entered a new phase. Membership in the U.N. General Assembly has increased by 28 (from 157 to 185) since 1990. This sudden increase compares in scale with the post–World War II spate of new states that was one result of the end of the colonial period.

Political movements today are defined more by ethnicity than by political ideology or territory. Many of the "isms" that dominated the twentieth century, including fascism and communism, are discredited, as are lesser creeds such as Arab radicalism and pan-Arabism. One result is that various groups are turning their energies inward, against populations within their borders. Such struggles are fast becoming commonplace.[35] The end to Europe's division and the demise of the Warsaw Pact provided an opportunity for Yugoslavs to redress long-held grievances. Similar "sorting out" of ethnic, political, and geographic questions can be seen in the former Soviet empire. The consequence is not only cross-border conflict but also conflicts within former states or parts of them (often themselves new states), frequently resulting in massive flows of refugees and human suffering on a major scale. Lebanon,

Rwanda, Burundi, northern Iraq, Bosnia, and Liberia are emblematic of this sort of situation, which tends to be awful in and of itself and easily a cause of wider regional conflict. The renewed strength of nationalist pulls is an important if dark dimension of deregulation.

One other change affecting the position of existing states deserves mention here: the diminution of the concept of sovereignty. For hundreds of years, the state system and international order rested on the notion that the state has a monopoly of authority within its borders and that it is a hostile act for one state to get involved uninvited in the internal affairs of another. The concept is so basic that it is enshrined in the U.N. Charter. Even so, the monopoly of the state within its own borders began to erode at about the same time the U.N. Charter was drafted, with the rise of the human rights movement. The idea began to take hold that citizens as well as states have rights, and that there are limits to what governments can legitimately do to their own people. Even more significant is the increased currency of the idea of humanitarian intervention, that outsiders possess the right or even duty to intervene in situations of mass suffering caused by either repressive or failed regimes. This change is both regulating (in its establishment of norms) and deregulating (in its potential to cause conflict). Overall, though, the diminution of sovereignty contributes more to deregulation: the old consensus is weakened but no new notion has taken its place.

Further contributing to (and reflecting) the weakening of the nation-state is the blurring of what is domestic and what is foreign. Borders count for less. The ability of any society to insulate itself from turmoil is limited. The Japanese subway gassing and Oklahoma City bombing of April 1995, like the World Trade Center bombing two years prior, show how modern societies are highly vulnerable to those possessing modern weapons. In the future, we will have to contend not only with such groups but also with rogue states that possess unconventional tools—chemical, biological, even nuclear weapons—and the means to deliver them across great distances.

The decline in American security shows up in others ways. Borders are increasingly under pressure from large numbers of immigrants. Drugs cannot be kept out no matter how many Coast Guard ships are sent to sea. The same goes for disease or environmental catastrophe: we are too connected by modern transport, too dependent upon a common atmosphere and ocean, to insulate ourselves from what others do or suffer from. Governments, particularly those of relatively open societies such as the United States, can limit what crosses their borders, but they cannot control entry or exit, much less seal themselves off.

All this is deregulating (and worrisome) for two reasons. These "external" phenomena can be difficult or impossible to prevent or manage, while several of them can lead to conflict. Refugee flows can destabilize societies; just as important, attempts to cut off flows have led to interventions, be it by India against Pakistan a quarter of a century ago or by the United States in Haiti much more recently. Military force has been used against drugs, both to eradicate the source and to interdict. One could imagine countries going to war over man-made environmental problems that spilled over borders. The list could go on; the point is that new sources of friction between states are not hard to come by despite the international treaties and other arrangements in effect.

LIBERALISM TRIUMPHANT

The prominence of societies that are largely if not entirely democratic and more rather than less market-oriented constitutes a third cardinal feature of this era. At no time in history have so many countries met these tests. If history has not ended, in this sense at least it has improved.

Why has this shift taken place? To some extent it reflects the inherent appeal of democracy and democratic ideas. It also reflects the greater embrace of capitalism (and the rejection of communism) and the reality that economic liberalization often reinforces pressures for political reform. Behind these changes is the fact that modern technology has made it more difficult for even totalitarian societies to keep out unwanted ideas and for statist economies to compete in the global marketplace.

Whatever the causes, a strong case can be made that the development is to be welcomed. Democracies are inherently desirable in the priority they accord individual freedoms and rights. Similarly, market economies have demonstrated a clear superiority in providing for the material needs of their citizens. In addition, relations between mature democracies tend to be better than relations between democracies and nondemocracies or among nondemocracies. The resort to force is simply less common.

But neither democracy nor market economics is a panacea that promises to regulate international relations. Developing or immature democracies can be vulnerable to mass prejudices and easily manipulated—and therefore prone to irresponsibility and violence. Moreover, new democracies are inherently fragile and can revert to something more authoritarian. We are already seeing signs of this throughout the formerly Communist areas of Europe and in Latin America.[36] Market economies can be prone to protectionist sentiments as their very openness ensures unending transition in which there will be losers. Most important, a good many countries are stopping short of effecting complete democracies or markets. They maintain (and are likely to over time) a greater degree of state involvement than is the custom in the American or British experience. The result is that the good often thought to emanate from such systems may not be as abundant. Overall, then, the trends in the direction of democracy and markets will promote regulation, but in and of themselves they are inadequate to ensure restraint and stability. Moreover, struggling democracies may be prone to instability at home and violence abroad. Again, deregulation will be the prevailing result.

DEREGULATION: A BALANCE SHEET

What, then, are we to make of the era of deregulation? It is relatively simple to identify positive and negative developments. The former would include a much reduced threat of all-out nuclear war; progress in resolving long-standing conflicts in southern Africa, the Middle East, and Northern Ireland; an end to communism; an increase in the number of societies that are more rather than less democratic and market-oriented; a greater flow of information; and the expansion of a liberal trade order.

At the same time, this age has worrisome aspects. Any such list would include an increased demand for protectionist trade measures; growing forced and illegal migration; proliferation of conventional and unconventional arms; heightened nationalism along ethnic and religious lines, including the rise of fundamentalist Islam; frequent local conflicts; increased power and activity by criminal organizations, drug cartels, and terrorist groups; and a decrease in U.S. willingness to support an active world role.

There are in addition to all the above simply those characteristics with significance that cannot be easily described as positive or negative. Here one would point to the decline in the prominence of the nation-state, the globalization of the economy, and the weakening of former blocs and alliances.

What of the future? What does the age of deregulation hold? The answer to this question reveals sharp disagreement. On one side of the divide are those who are relatively sanguine if not downright optimistic. To bolster their case, they make a number of arguments: the declining utility of military force and hence the reduced likelihood of great-power military conflict, the belief that heightened economic interdependence constitutes a bulwark against instability because countries benefiting from trade will do nothing to upset the source of their mutual gain, the historical record that democracies tend not to fight other democracies, and the absence of any "revolutionary" great power that seeks and has the strength to overthrow the existing order.

Each of these insights has merit. But neither individually nor collectively do they justify the conclusion that the post–Cold War era is likely to be relatively stable. To begin with, it is impossible to rule out great-power military conflict. One can easily imagine the United States and China clashing over Taiwan, or, with time, the United States and Russia over Ukraine, China and Russia over Mongolia or Siberia, or Japan and China over some regional question. Even more possible are conflicts involving one great power and a medium-sized adversary. Wars can occur and be costly without becoming total struggles of annihilation or conquest; indeed, the fact that nuclear weapons place a premium on avoiding escalation suggests that limited war may once again emerge as a possibility. John Mueller's judgment, "For the last two or three centuries major war—war among developed countries—has moved toward terminal disrepute because of its perceived repulsiveness and futility," may apply to most of Western Europe and Latin America, but it is premature as a general proposition, as is Richard Rosecrance's judgment that "Wars of aggression and wars of punishment are losing their impact and justification."[37]

Economic interdependence does build incentives to cooperate in that all parties are better off if they do. But interdependence offers no insurance against major disagreements or conflicts; if it did, neither world war should have broken out. Trade disputes could well trigger protectionist reactions. Also, raw material exporters and importers could come to blows over matters of price or supply. Migration has already shown itself able to cause conflict between states. Even the environment is a potential casus belli. Similarly, democracy will not guarantee harmony in those cases where the democracy is immature (as in the former Yugoslavia) or when the embrace of democracy is incomplete (throughout much of Asia). Also, it is clear that important countries have resisted the lure of democratic reform—and that some that are currently democratic may not always be that way.

In the wake of the Soviet Union no great power seeks hegemony over the current international order or a very different one. As one observer noted, "Today, despite increased surface turbulence, the international system is structurally sound because none of the great powers seeks a hegemonic role in the international system."[38] But several countries, including China and Russia, are potential revolutionary states in their regions. Just as important, a significant number of other actors—Iran, Iraq, North Korea, Libya, terrorist groups—do want to change the existing order in their respective regions and have the means to attempt to do so.

The absence of a clear, two-party struggle for global hegemony has had another effect: increased potential for lesser conflicts. "Strategic detachment" is a reality. Great powers no longer have as much need or incentive to act in a specific crisis for fear of losing ground in any global struggle. Intrinsic interests matter more than those that are ascribed. It makes it easier to see events in isolation—and, as a result, to allow them to happen or even fester, as has often been the case in Africa. At the same time, it means that instabilities can erupt with only local effects; the potential for the spreading of crises is much reduced. As a result, in a deregulated world the prospects for global conflict appear reduced while those for local conflict are enhanced.[39] The one exception might be the Middle East, where long-term recipients of Soviet largesse such as the PLO and Syria have shown a greater interest in political compromise now that their traditional source of support has ended.

But the principal reason it is difficult to embrace strong optimism about what deregulation will entail is the sheer dynamism of the current period of international relations. For any system to enjoy stability, two things are required. First, there must be a balance of strength so that no single member is tempted to try to dominate the others. Second, some consensus is needed over the means and desirability (and direction) of change. These twin standards make for a tall test. What is required is not simply a mechanical balance of power in the Newtonian sense but agreement on the rules and purposes of international relations. It is a "concert"—or what Henry Kissinger described as "legitimacy," the result of international agreement about the permissible aims and methods of foreign policy. With such agreement, stability is a realistic aim; without it, it is not.[40]

The challenge of maintaining a military balance will tend to grow over time, as weapons proliferate and countries translate their wealth into military power. The challenge for the United States of building a concert appears even greater. American ideas about human rights, democracy, and the market are not always admired or accepted. Active promotion of human rights, to cite one example, is inconsistent with the principle of noninterference in a state's internal affairs, one of the five pillars of Chinese foreign policy. U.S. primacy, much less hegemony, is not universally desired by states as diverse as China, Russia, France, and Iran. Not everyone is ready to sign on to using military force (or ruling it out) in the same set of circumstances, backing sanctions, or supporting humanitarian interventions. The permanent five in the U.N. Security Council—the United States, Britain, France, China, and Russia—often disagree with one another and are likely to do so more rather than less, given political trends in Russia, Chinese-American differences on a wealth of issues from Taiwan to trade, and the weakening of transatlantic ties. Bringing in Japan and Germany—in effect, trying to make a concert out of an expanded version of the countries that attend the annual G-7 summit—would make reaching consensus only that much more difficult.[41] Moreover, such a grouping would still exclude a number of states that are dominant in their respective regions, including India, Brazil, Israel, and South Africa.

The result is that the notion of a standing concert of powers that would regulate post–Cold War international relations is far-fetched.[42] Terrorists, rogue states, medium powers, and would-be great powers will resist endorsing the American vision of world order in selected instances. If and when they do, the United States will face a choice. History demonstrates that international consensus emerges either voluntarily, when parties subscribe to a set of norms because they realize they are better off if they do, or because reluctant members of the international community are forced to go along. Thus, what will prove crucial is the ability of the United States to persuade others to adopt and abide by its preferences—and the will and the ability of the United States to act as a sheriff, to mobilize itself and others to insist on them when resistance emerges. This, more than anything else, will determine the character of the age of deregulation.

NOTES

1. James Atlas, "Name that Era: Pinpointing a Moment on the Map of History," *New York Times*, May 19, 1995, E1, E5.
2. James N. Rosenau, "Muddling, Meddling and Modelling: Alternative Approaches to the Study of World Politics in an Era of Rapid Change," *Millennium* 8, no. 2 (August 1979), 134.

3. Francis Fukuyama, "The End of History," *National Interest*, no. 16 (Summer 1989), 3–18. Fukuyama developed his ideas further in his *The End of History and the Last Man* (New York: Free Press, 1992).

4. John J. Mearsheimer, "Back to the Future: Instability in Europe After the Cold War," *International Security* 15, no. 1 (Summer 1990), 5–56.

5. Robert D. Kaplan, "The Coming Anarchy," *Atlantic* (February 1994), 44–76. Kaplan subsequently expanded his ideas in a book, *The Ends of the Earth: A Journey at the Dawn of the Twenty-First Century* (New York: Random House, 1996).

6. Samuel P. Huntington, *The Clash of Civilizations and the Remaking of World Order* (New York: Simon & Schuster, 1996), 125. These themes were first introduced by Huntington in an article titled "The Clash of Civilizations?" published in *Foreign Affairs* in the summer of 1993 (volume 72, no. 3, 22–49). Huntington clearly gained confidence in the correctness of his views over the years: the question mark that accompanied the title in the article was dropped for the book.

7. See, for example, Charles Krauthammer, "The Unipolar Moment," *Foreign Affairs* 70, no. 1 ("America and the World, 1990/91"), 23–33, and Zalmay M. Khalilzad, *From Containment to Global Leadership? America and the World After the Cold War* (Santa Monica, Cal.: RAND, 1995).

8. See, for example, Janne E. Nolan (ed.), *Global Engagement: Cooperation and Security in the 21st Century* (Washington, D.C.: Brookings, 1994), as well as Richard Rosecrance, "A New Concert of Powers," *Foreign Affairs* 71, no. 2 (Spring 1992), 64–83.

9. Kenichi Omae, *The End of the Nation State* (New York: Free Press, 1995).

10. G. John Ikenberry, "The Myth of Post–Cold War Chaos," *Foreign Affairs* 75, no. 3 (May/June 1996), 79–91.

11. See Benjamin R. Barber, "Jihad vs. McWorld," *Atlantic* (March 1992), 53–63. This was later expanded into a book by the same name (New York: Times Books, 1995). Also see John Lewis Gaddis, "Toward the Post–Cold War World," in Eugene R. Wittkopf (ed.), *The Future of American Foreign Policy*, 2nd ed. (New York: St. Martin's, 1994), 16–36, and Joseph A. Camilleri and Jim Falk, *The End of Sovereignty? The Politics of a Shrinking and Fragmenting World* (Aldershot, U.K.: E. Elgar, 1992).

12. See Max Singer and Aaron Wildavsky, *The Real World Order: Zones of Peace/Zones of Turmoil* (Chatham, N.J.: Chatham House, 1993).

13. Ironically, it is Huntington who provides one of the best repudiations of Fukuyama. Fouad Ajami, meanwhile, has provided a strong rebuttal to Huntington. See Samuel Huntington, "The Errors of Endism," *National Interest*, no. 17 (Fall 1989), 3–11, and Fouad Ajami, "The Summoning," *Foreign Affairs* 72, no. 4 (September–October, 1993), 2–9. Huntington's response to Ajami and other critics, "If Not Civilizations, What?" is in *Foreign Affairs* 72, no. 5 (November–December, 1993), 186–194.

14. For a useful discussion of the impact of airline deregulation, see Adam Bryant, "On a Wing and a Fare: Deregulation Decoded," *New York Times*, November 5, 1995, E5. The definitive work on the subject is Steven A. Mor-

rison and Clifford Winston, *The Evolution of the Aviation Industry* (Washington, D.C.: Brookings, 1995). A more recent assessment of the impact of deregulation on the airline industry can be found in Robert Crandall and Jerry Ellig, *Economic Deregulation and Customer Choice: Lessons for the Electric Industry* (Fairfax, Va.: Center For Market Processes, 1997), 34–47.

15. Thomas S. Kuhn, *The Structure of Scientific Revolutions* (Chicago: University of Chicago Press, 1970), 17.

16. Charles Krauthammer, "The Unipolar Moment," *Foreign Affairs* 70, no. 1 ("America and the World, 1990/91"), 23–33.

17. Aaron L. Friedberg, "The Future of American Power," *Political Science Quarterly* 109, no. 1 (1994), 21.

18. See Richard Halloran, "The Rising East," *Foreign Policy*, no. 102 (Spring 1996), 3–21.

19. This is the central theme of Paul Kennedy's important book, *The Rise and Fall of the Great Powers: Economic Change and Military Conflict from 1500 to 2000* (New York: Random House, 1987).

20. Robert Gilpin, *War and Change in World Politics* (Cambridge: Cambridge University Press, 1981), 13.

21. See Aaron L. Friedberg, "Ripe for Rivalry: Prospects for Peace in a Multipolar Asia," *International Security* 18, no. 3 (Winter 1993/94), 5–33.

22. For a country-by-country breakdown of the status of unconventional weapons programs, see Office of the Secretary of Defense, *Proliferation: Threat and Response* (Washington, D.C.: U.S. Government Printing Office, 1996).

23. *The Weapons Proliferation Threat* (Washington, D.C.: Central Intelligence Agency, March 1995). Also see Leonard S. Spector and Mark G. McDonough, *Tracking Nuclear Proliferation: A Guide in Maps and Charts, 1995* (Washington, D.C.: Carnegie Endowment for International Peace, 1995) and Office of Technology Assessment, *Proliferation of Weapons of Mass Destruction: Assessing the Risks* (Washington, D.C.: U.S. Government Printing Office, 1993).

24. See Graham T. Allison et al., *Avoiding Nuclear Anarchy: Containing the Threat of Loose Nuclear Weapons and Fissile Material* (Cambridge, Mass.: MIT Press, 1996).

25. For some background on the evolving nuclear proliferation problem, see Leonard S. Spector, *Nuclear Ambitions: The Spread of Nuclear Weapons 1989–1990* (Washington, D.C.: Carnegie Endowment for International Peace, 1990); Robert D. Blackwill and Albert Carnesale (eds.), *New Nuclear Nations: Consequences for U.S. Policy* (New York: Council on Foreign Relations, 1993); Zachary S. Davis and Benjamin Frankel (eds.), *The Proliferation Puzzle: Why Nuclear Weapons Spread (and What Results)*, Security Studies 2, Nos. 3/4 (Spring/Summer 1993); and Brad Roberts, *Weapons Proliferation and World Order After the Cold War* (Hague: Kluwer Law International, 1996).

26. See the arguments of Kenneth N. Waltz in the book he coauthored with Scott D. Sagan, *The Spread of Nuclear Weapons: A Debate* (New York: Norton, 1995). In this book, Sagan argues the traditional view against proliferation. For another nonconformist approach, see Doug Bandow, "Let 'Em Have

Nukes," *New York Times Magazine*, November 13, 1994, 56–57. A good review of this debate can be found in David J. Karl, "Proliferation Pessimism and Emerging Nuclear Powers," *International Security* 21, no. 3 (Winter 1996/97), 87–119.

27. John J. Mearsheimer, "The Case for a Ukrainian Nuclear Deterrent," *Foreign Affairs* 72, no. 3 (Summer 1993), 50–66.

28. The quotation is from Barber, *Jihad vs. McWorld* (New York: Times Books, 1995), 23. There are actually two books with virtually the same title, the difference being a hyphen: Jean-Marie Guehenno, *The End of the Nation-State* (Minneapolis: University of Minnesota Press, 1995) and Kenichi Omae, *The End of the Nation State* (New York: Free Press, 1995).

29. *Daedalus* 124, no. 2 (Spring 1995).

30. The notion of the state coexisting with other actors is in itself nothing new. More than two decades ago Seyom Brown wrote of global society being a "polyarchy" involving states, subnational groups, and transnational interests. See his *New Forces in World Politics* (Washington, D.C.: Brookings, 1974). What has changed, though, is the increased number and power of nonnational entities. See Jessica T. Mathews, "Power Shift," *Foreign Affairs* 76, no. 1 (January/February 1997), 50–66.

31. See Ethan B. Kapstein, "We Are Us," *National Interest*, no. 26 (Winter 1991–92), 55–62. Also see Louis W. Pauly and Simon Reich, "National Structures and Multinational Corporate Behavior: Enduring Differences in the Age of Globalization," *International Organization* 51, no. 1 (Winter 1997), 1–30.

32. For a similar view, see two pieces in the *Economist*: "The Myth of the Powerless State," October 7, 1995, 15–16, and "The Nation-State Is Dead; Long Live the Nation-State," December 23, 1995–January 5, 1996, 15–18. Also see my somewhat outdated but still largely accurate "The Primacy of the State . . . or Revising the Revisionists," *Daedalus* 108, no. 4 (Fall 1979), 125–138.

33. This is not to suggest that some are not trying. Syria reportedly bans modems and places a high tax on fax machines to discourage their use. China has promulgated regulations requiring that any use of the Internet be on a government-approved channel. See Seth Falon, "Chinese Tiptoe into Internet, Wary of Watchdogs," *New York Times*, February 5, 1996, A3.

34. Jessica T. Mathews, "Power Shift," *Foreign Affairs* 76, no. 1 (January/February 1997), 51.

35. On this theme see Hans Magnus Enzensberger, *Civil Wars: From L.A. to Bosnia* (New York: New Press, 1994); Daniel P. Moynihan, *Pandaemonium: Ethnicity in International Politics* (New York: Oxford University Press, 1993); and Anthony D. Smith, "The Ethnic Sources of Nationalism," *Survival* 35, no. 1 (Spring 1993), 48–62.

36. See Thomas Carothers, "Democracy Without Illusions," *Foreign Affairs* 76, no. 1 (January/February 1997), 85–99.

37. John Mueller, *Retreat from Doomsday: The Obsolescence of Major War* (New York: Basic Books, 1989), 4. Also see Richard Rosecrance, "The Rise of the Virtual State," *Foreign Affairs* 75, no. 4 (July/August 1996), 58. En-

dorsement of this thesis can be found from Carl Kaysen, "Is War Obsolete? A Review Essay," *International Security* 14, no. 4 (Spring 1990), 42–64. One effective critique is John J. Mearsheimer, "Back to the Future: Instability in Europe After the Cold War," *International Security* 15, no. 1 (Summer 1990), 5–56.

38. See C. William Maynes, "The New Pessimism," *Foreign Policy,* no. 100 (Fall 1995), 44.

39. Robert J. Samuelson, "End of the Third World," *Washington Post,* July 18, 1990, A23.

40. Henry A. Kissinger, *A World Restored: The Politics of Conservatism in a Revolutionary Age* (New York: Grosset & Dunlap, 1964), 1.

41. G-7 members are the United States, Canada, France, Great Britain, Italy, Germany, and Japan. European (EU) leaders are also invited, as is Russia on most occasions.

42. Examples of such advocacy are William E. Odom, "How to Create a True World Order," *Orbis* 39, no. 2 (Spring 1995), 155–172; Richard Rosecrance, "A New Concert of Powers," *Foreign Affairs* 71, no. 2 (Spring 1992), 64–83; and Zbigniew Brzezinski, "Let's Add 4 to the G-7," *New York Times,* June 25, 1996, A21.

Chapter 3

A Doctrine of Regulation

The age of deregulation will be a time of great change, including rising and falling powers, a large number of small conflicts, considerable shifts in wealth, and new technologies that will both enhance and endanger our lives. The question naturally arises: What are the most pressing U.S. interests in such a world? An illustrative list (in no particular order) might include protecting U.S. territory and American citizens from attack; controlling access to U.S. territory against illegal drugs and immigrants, as well as disease; preventing the emergence of a hostile superpower; avoiding the domination of Europe, the Asia-Pacific, the Persian Gulf, and/or the Caribbean littoral by a hostile power; reducing existing inventories of weapons of mass destruction and lesser arms; preventing the spread and/or use of weapons of mass destruction; maintaining an open trading order; discouraging the use of force in international affairs and encouraging the peaceful resolution of conflicts; promoting U.S. exports; safeguarding Israel's security; maintaining a functioning international monetary system; guaranteeing access to needed energy supplies and other raw materials; fostering democracy, human rights, and market economic reforms; safeguarding the global environment against severe degradation; and preventing genocide or mass suffering.

Other interests could no doubt be added while some might deserve to be subtracted. What is most noteworthy, though, is both how little U.S. interests have changed since the end of the Cold War (or World War II, for that matter) and how extensive they remain. Rather, what has changed the most are the threats, which are arguably greater in number and smaller in scale. Indeed, as a rule of thumb, threats tend to change more quickly than a country's interests, which tend to be enduring and change slowly if at all.

Formulating and implementing a foreign policy to protect and promote American interests will prove difficult, in part because there is no obvious, much less accepted, answer to what constitutes American priorities. The absence of any such answer is not the result of a lack of intellectual effort but the inherent difficulty of the problem. Determining priorities for policy—designing a foreign policy doctrine—involves a complex, three-way calculation of national interests, likely opportunities, and emerging threats.

First, it is necessary to identify and weigh U.S. interests. All are not equal in value: some interests are vital, others simply important or modest. All such judgments are unavoidably subjective and controversial, although the importance of an interest must be directly related to its bearing on the country's political freedom, physical safety, and economic prosperity. My list for America's vital interests is thus no hostile domination of Europe, the Asia-Pacific, and/or the Persian Gulf; denial of a nuclear weapons capability to rogue actors; maintenance of Mexican and Caribbean stability as well as functioning relationships with these areas and Canada; protection of U.S. territory from attack; sustaining open trade and working monetary regimes; and prevention or protection against a major threat posed by the global environment.[1]

There is a temptation to include a great many interests as vital. Like most temptations, this one ought to be avoided. Vital interests are those with the greatest potential to affect what is the most basic. Important and minor interests have correspondingly less potential to affect our security, prosperity, and freedom and, especially in the case of minor or peripheral interests, often reflect preferences as much as anything.

Contrary to what is often posited, a willingness to use military force is *not* an indication that an interest is vital, any more than a reluctance to use force suggests an interest is minor. Military force is simply one instrument of policy, and its selection reflects its utility relative to other policy tools. There will thus be times when U.S. military action would be unwise despite enormous stakes, say, in resisting a revolution that comes to threaten a critical ally such as Egypt or Saudi Arabia, just as there will be instances when force might be warranted even though the interests involved are relatively modest, as in some vast humanitarian crisis in Africa. Indeed, one of the hallmarks of a great power is a willingness and an ability to use military force even when the interests at stake are less than vital.

Second, identifying and weighing interests, however necessary and difficult, is not sufficient. Policy must also take into account the potential to promote these interests. Promoting democracy and human rights may be important interests, but U.S. foreign policy can only rarely accomplish this. The same can be said for bringing peace to the Middle East or Northern Ireland. Something must be doable as well as desirable. If something is not feasible, then it cannot be a foreign policy priority, even less the basis of much of what the United States does in the world.

Third, it is necessary for policy to assess threats, i.e., the requirement to protect interests. The security of our borders is certainly a high interest, but where there is no threat there is no need to act. Thus, we do not place large armies along our borders with either Canada or Mexico, even though the United States would be affected significantly were either to become a failed state or come under the sway of a leadership hostile to the United States. The debate over whether to field a national defense against ballistic missiles hinges in large part over such questions as what kind of ballistic missile threat will materialize and when, and whether U.S. technology is likely to be effective against it. Again, the obvious interest in self-protection does not automatically lead to a change in policy (and a decision to deploy missile defenses) unless the threat emerges and can be reduced meaningfully by what we do.

Such a three-way calculation of interests, opportunity (or feasibility), and threats is complex and difficult, but it is necessary. Hiding behind facile formulations of "selective engagement" that provide neither the criteria for selection nor the means of engagement is not enough. More than anything else, the determination of priorities is the beginning of foreign policy. Such a determination goes to the core of choosing a doctrine, something necessary to help clarify priorities and to build popular support for sustaining such an orientation.

Why is such a process necessary? There is an unavoidable gap between what a country seeks and what it can afford. Only by deciding priorities—in effect, by deciding what we are willing to do without—is it possible to allocate resources intelligently. Priorities also allow us to size, shape, and deploy our military forces, design and focus our intelligence community, direct our foreign assistance, and train and assign our diplomats. Only by determining priorities do we have a basis for deciding what to do when more than one interest is at stake at one time and something has to give.

Proof that this is easier said than done is the existence of no fewer than six competing foreign policy doctrines for the United States, all vying to replace containment and animate U.S. foreign policy in the age of deregulation.[2] They represent the serious universe of choice, and individually or, more likely, in some combination are certain to provide direction for the next phase of American foreign policy.

HEGEMONY

The notion of primacy, or hegemony, has already been introduced above in the descriptive sense, i.e., that in the post–Cold War world, the United States enjoys a status of first among unequals. This is true not only militarily but economically and politically as well.

As a foreign policy priority or doctrine, however, hegemony means something very different. A doctrine of hegemony is prescriptive. It would make the goal of U.S. foreign policy the maintenance of relative advantage. It would seek to prolong the unipolar moment and make it an era.

Hegemony (sometimes described as unipolarity) was the preferred goal of the "Pentagon Paper," a working document of the Bush administration's Defense Department. Leaked to the media in early 1992, the draft planning document declared that "Our first objective is to prevent the re-emergence of a new rival, either on the territory of the former Soviet Union or elsewhere, that poses a threat on the order of that posed formerly by the Soviet Union. . . . Our strategy must now refocus on precluding the emergence of any potential future global competitor."[3]

Why would such a goal make sense? It would by definition prevent the emergence of a new adversary or adversaries that could not only threaten U.S. interests but destroy the United States. "It is in our national interest that no other superpower emerge whose political and social values are profoundly hostile to our own," writes one observer.[4] More recently, Robert Kagan and William Kristol suggested that "American hegemony is the only reliable defense against a breakdown of peace and international order. The appropriate goal of American foreign policy, therefore, is to preserve that hegemony as far into the future as possible."[5]

Less dramatically, a doctrine of hegemony could prevent the evolution of a much more complicated and less stable world composed of several independent great (but not necessarily hostile) powers. Charles Krauthammer argues just this point: "If America's allies believe that they can rely on American power, they will have no reason to turn themselves into military superpowers. . . . the alternative to unipolarity is not a stable, static multipolar world. It is not an eighteenth-century world in which mature powers like Europe, Russia, China, America and Japan jockey for position in the game of nations. The alternative to unipolarity is chaos."[6] Thus, unipolarity is seen by its advocates as preferable not simply to bipolarity but to multipolarity as well.[7]

For better or worse, such a goal is beyond our reach. It simply is not doable. As Kenneth Waltz has pointed out, "For a country not to become a great power is a structural anomaly. . . . Sooner or later, usually sooner, the international status of countries has risen in step with their material resources. Countries with great power economies have become great powers, whether or not reluctantly."[8] In the cases of Japan and Germany—"anomalies" given the legacy of World War II and its impact on domestic political culture—American activism can make less likely and slow their emergence as military powers. It cannot, however, prevent such an outcome forever. The future of these countries will depend mostly on their own perception of national interests, threats, political culture, and economic strength.

More to the point, there is no way the United States can ensure that Russia does not re-create a massive threat or that some future Chinese government will not decide to challenge the United States for regional or even global predominance. The most we can do with any certainty is slow another country's economic and military growth—and then with only the most modest of effects—by denying technology or markets. But all the U.S. denial in the world will count for little, given what others (be they governments, firms, or criminal groups) will be prepared to provide and what countries can do for themselves. Preventive military strikes are an option only for destroying specific, limited capabilities of an adversary. Such strikes are risky even at that, and out of the question when the adversary has a large military capability and a broad capacity to regenerate or retaliate. Quite simply, while it is within the reach of the United States to continue as a great power and to affect the behavior of other powers, it is beyond our ability to prevent another country from joining the ranks of the great.

A related problem with a doctrine of hegemony is cost. Kristol and Kagan, two advocates of this approach, estimate that the annual increase required in defense spending alone would be between $60 and $80 billion.[9] Moreover, the demands of perpetuating primacy will grow at a time when Americans are less inclined to pay the price. If history is any guide, Americans will consider paying a much larger price for national security only if we feel our vital interests clearly threatened. Hegemony is merely one approach to avoiding reaching such a juncture. It would be better to accomplish this same task by enlisting the collective efforts of others. To return to an economic metaphor, what matters more than America's share of the geopolitical market is our profitability, and there are less costly alternatives to hegemony that promise results for U.S. national security that are as good or better.

Questions about hegemony should not be interpreted as opposition to American leadership. Leadership, however, requires followers, and while there are many purposes for which the United States can generate international support, maintaining American primacy is not one of them. Indeed, a doctrine of hegemony is likely to stimulate resistance.[10] Any foreign policy doctrine must appeal to multiple audiences, not just the domestic, if it is to succeed. Hegemony fails this test.

ISOLATIONISM

If hegemony is at one end of the spectrum of potential choices, isolationism falls at the other. An isolationist doctrine would produce a minimal foreign policy that would be circumscribed in its goals, restrained in what it did, and modest in what it required in resources.

Contemporary isolationism stems from several wellsprings. First, there are those who believe that the United States *need not* be active in the world owing to a lack of vital interests or imminent threats. Second, there are those who argue that the United States *should not* be overly ambitious, either because of the intractable nature of many of the world's problems or the belief that U.S. involvement will tend only to exacerbate them. Third, there are those who maintain that the United States *cannot* afford to be active in the world because of pressing domestic priorities and limited resources. As might be expected, some people subscribe to all or some combination of these positions.[11]

One necessary question is whether those attracted to a posture of isolationism (or, less pejoratively, minimalism) are correct in their assessment that, in the age of deregulation, the United States has to contend with relatively modest interests and threats. In one important way at least, threats are significantly reduced.

We no longer live in a world in which a rival possesses missiles aimed at us with the capacity to destroy us in an instant. Nor is the United States engaged any longer in a global struggle for influence or advantage. We won, and the other side not only lost but disappeared. The challenge posed by fundamentalist Islam, while significant, is largely confined to the Middle East and Persian Gulf. No strategic or ideological challenger is capable of waging a global competition. As Jonathan Clarke has written, "Today's wars (Bosnia, Angola, Armenia–Azerbaijan, the antinarcotics battle, among others) and today's problems (ethnic upheaval, religious intolerance, terrorism, economic imbalances, fragile democracies) do not provide the all-encompassing challenge that was inherent in totalitarian fascism and communism."[12]

But this perspective is not sufficient; on the contrary, it tends to underestimate the interests we do have and the threats arrayed against them. Beyond any moral obligations or philosophical commitments stemming from humanitarian and political considerations, there are still potential problems in the world—crises in the Persian Gulf or northeast Asia, a breakdown of trade, a renewed Russian threat to Europe, a Chinese bid for regional hegemony, the proliferation of weapons of mass destruction, terrorist attacks, and so on—that could directly and dramatically affect U.S. well-being at home. A number of factors, including economic globalization, ease of travel, and the growing range of weapons, tend to make it more difficult for the United States or any other country to insulate itself. With such high "connectivity," there is no apparent shortage of interests or potential threats.

There is, however, a related argument, that we can do little about the state of the world. Ronald Steel, for example, urges Americans to "get over the superpower syndrome" and accept the reality that "there are a good many problems for which there may be no solution at all."[13] Alan Tonelson writes that "foreign policy is not an end in itself but a means to a highly specific end: enhancing the safety and prosperity of the American people. A domestic focus is imperative not in order to rebuild the foundation of American world leadership but to prepare America for a world that cannot be led or stabilized or organized in any meaningful sense of these words."[14]

The problem with this perspective is that it ignores what we can usefully do. U.S. diplomacy alone cannot bring peace to the Middle East, but it can facilitate the process. U.S. arms can deter conflict in the Persian Gulf and the Korean peninsula and protect U.S. interests and restore stability if deterrence fails. Action by the United States can keep millions of people alive who would otherwise be victims of civil war or hunger, as was the case in Somalia. Bosnia offers a graphic example of what is likely to happen when the United States stands aloof—as compared to when it not only engages but leads, as it did in the summer of 1995.

The theme most central to the minimalist, or neo-isolationist, perspective, however, is the economic: the cost of our national security effort—defense, intelligence, assistance, diplomacy, and so on—is one we can ill afford. Most minimalists see the United States in social and economic decline, in part because of the costs of decades of international activism. With the Cold War won, they favor shifting resources to domestic needs, as William Hyland makes clear: "The United States has never been less threatened by foreign forces than it is today. But the unfortunate corollary is that never since the Great Depression has the threat to domestic well-being been greater. By winning the Cold War . . . we have earned about a decade of freedom to reorient our foreign policy and concentrate our resources, energy and attention on dealing with the domestic crisis."[15] Such views are intellectually consistent with the writings of Paul Kennedy, the influential historian who attributes the decline of great powers throughout history to "imperial overstretch," his phrase for spending too much on a world role and not enough at home.[16]

It is possible to discern evidence of isolationism in Congress, including widespread and often reflexive opposition to uses of military force and to funding several tools of foreign policy, notably assistance and diplomacy. One sees isolationism in the conservative politics of Patrick Buchanan, in the independent "reform" movement of H. Ross Perot, and in the left wing of the

Democratic Party. It has also been one tendency of the Clinton presidency. Minimalist rhetoric dominated many of the statements of the 1992 presidential campaign—as symbolized by candidate Clinton's promise, if elected, to focus like a laser beam on domestic issues. Once in office, President Clinton continued to be swayed by minimalist concerns. The lure of minimalism was apparent not simply by what the administration said and did but even more by what it did *not* say or do. It was as much as anything the lack of attention on foreign policy that reflected a minimalist impulse. This bias helps to explain the reluctance to get involved seriously in either Bosnia or Rwanda and in the decision to exit from Somalia as soon as substantial costs materialized. The stated rationale (by then Under Secretary of State Peter Tarnoff in May 1993) was that U.S. activism in the world would have to be scaled back because of resource constraints.[17] The unarticulated aim seemed to be to avoid the fate of Lyndon Johnson, whose plans for a Great Society foundered in the jungles and hamlets of Vietnam.

These and similar arguments fail to convince for two reasons. On the one hand, they exaggerate the real cost of national security; on the other, they underestimate the contributions an active national security policy makes to domestic well-being.

A minimalist foreign policy would save some resources in the short run. The United States now spends nearly $300 billion a year on national security, including defense, intelligence, foreign assistance, diplomacy, and other international programs—a considerable sum by any measure. At the same time, it is necessary to place this figure in context. U.S. spending on national security represents approximately one-fifth of all federal spending. It is about the same as what we spend on discretionary civilian programs or Medicare, and less than we spend on Social Security. Spending on national security now comes to under 4 percent of GNP, less than half the level during the Kennedy administration and the lowest level at any time since the beginning of the Cold War.[18] The level of spending on defense and other tools of national security has been declining for over a decade, since midway through the Reagan presidency.

A DOCTRINE OF REGULATION

Moreover, it does not figure that spending less on national security will automatically add to prosperity. The United States experienced far higher rates of economic growth during the 1950s and 1960s, decades of far higher rates of spending on defense. Similarly, countries as different as China, South Korea, and Israel are proof that rapid economic growth and large-scale military expenditure (at percentages of GNP several times our own) can go hand in hand.

Nor is it at all obvious that spending less on defense would ease our domestic problems.[19] Many of them are not the result of lack of resources. It is doubtful that what most ails us at home—crime, illegitimacy, drug use, divorce, racism, and the like—would be fixed by further drawing down resources devoted to our presence abroad and shifting them to domestic purposes. It is even possible to argue that in some cases—welfare comes to mind—resources have exacerbated social problems. Even if more spending were needed in selected areas, a strong case could be made that needed funds could be provided simply by slowing the growth of entitlements such as Social Security and Medicare, which have continued to rise rapidly in cost and have not been reformed to take into account the real rate of inflation, the accumulation of wealth by many recipients, or the reality that Americans are on the average living longer.

Worse, over time a minimalist foreign policy could end up being more costly. Neglect will prove to be malign. Conflict on the Korean peninsula, for example, would disrupt trade and economic life throughout the region. There would be no way the United States could wall itself off from the effects. Successful terrorism against targets in the United States would exact a terrible human and financial toll. A failed Mexico or other collapsed states in the Western Hemisphere would increase immigration pressures on American territory. Hostile control of energy resources in the Persian Gulf could lead to higher prices for oil and gas and to temporary shortages. A posture of isolationism, whatever its near-term savings, could increase the likelihood that critical problems or threats to vital U.S. interests will emerge. U.S. reluctance to act may well encourage others to fill the perceived void. Arms proliferation would likely accelerate; aggression would almost certainly become more commonplace. If this occurred, the United States could well have no choice but to act—but in a context far less amenable to relatively inexpensive solutions. The notion that what the United States or any other country does overseas comes at the expense of what it could be doing at home is flawed; in a deregulated world in which the significance of borders is blurring and that of distance diminishing, foreign and domestic policy are increasingly two sides of the same coin.

None of this is intended as an argument for ignoring domestic problems or for avoiding desirable economic reforms. Not only do such matters merit attention and treatment in their own right, but U.S. foreign policy is directly affected in important ways by the U.S. domestic situation. Only a healthy and prosperous United States can preserve the economic and social foundations of international activism.[20] In addition, the example of a successful society and economy are powerful tools in the struggle for ideas around the world and in the effort to promote democracy and market economics. Some of the luster of the Gulf War accomplishment was tarnished, for example, by the impact of the Los Angeles riots, which presented a very different and markedly less attractive image of America to the rest of the world.

WILSONIANISM

This enduring and uniquely American approach to foreign policy reflects a desire to see other countries adopt a form of democratic governance and civil society that our own experience suggests is the best for both the individual and the community. The American conception of democracy and governance is based upon a Newtonian notion in which authority is distributed among separate and competing institutions so that individual liberty is protected. This philosophical preference is buttressed by a practical one, namely, that democracies tend to treat their own citizens with greater tolerance and are far less likely to resort to force in their relations with their fellow democracies. Moreover, established democracies are naturally less brittle and therefore less susceptible to radical and potentially disruptive change. A more democratic world, it is believed, will not only be inherently better but also more peaceful, stable, and prosperous.[21]

Democracy promotion needs to be understood as something broader than the promotion of human rights. The latter, a priority of the Carter administration, was more a focus on the behavior of governments, whereas a democracy-oriented posture seeks to transform the nature of societies. Such a systemic change can in principle be brought about directly by promoting institutional changes or indirectly through encouraging market economic reforms that tend to support forces in society seeking greater political pluralism.

The promotion of democracy constituted the principal attempt of the first Clinton administration to articulate a new foreign policy doctrine. National Security Advisor Anthony Lake argued in September 1993 that "the successor to a doctrine of containment must be a strategy of enlargement, the enlargement of the world's free community of market democracies."[22] Priority "targets" were the formerly Communist states of central and eastern Europe, the newly independent countries of the former Soviet Union, and the still developing or incomplete democracies of Latin America and Asia. By declaring democracy promotion to be so central, the Clinton administration placed itself squarely in the tradition of Woodrow Wilson and his early–twentieth-century quest. The emphasis is by no means limited to Democrats; Wilsonianism was a major element of Ronald Reagan's foreign policy and continues to be prominent in the writings of people normally described as neoconservatives and associated more with the Republican Party.[23]

There are several problems, however, with a doctrine of democracy promotion. Enlarging the community of democracies provides little or no policy-relevant guidance for dealing with a host of pressing problems, many of which cannot wait until the long-term process of democratization works its uncertain way. "Enlargement" was essentially irrelevant in helping the Clinton administration come to grips with Bosnia, Rwanda, North Korea, or Somalia.[24] In addition, the active promotion of democracy is a luxury policymakers can only sometimes afford. The United States arguably has little choice but to overlook a lack of democracy with friends (such as in the Persian Gulf) where other interests (such as energy and security) take precedence. For this reason, the Bush administration made Kuwait's liberation, not its embrace of democracy, an objective of Desert Storm.

At the same time, a foreign policy predicated on spreading democracy can be difficult to implement vis-à-vis our foes, either because we lack the means to influence them—it is difficult to penalize more than we do or, owing to important policy differences, impossible to offer inducements—or because, again, we have more pressing concerns. Thus, a democratic North Korea would be nice, but in the meantime we had better focus on Pyongyang's nuclear ambitions and the threat it poses to the South. Similarly, we would like to see China demonstrate greater respect for human rights, but for now we need China's help with North Korea while we seek access to China's enormous market and try to discourage Beijing from exporting nuclear weapons technology or using military force against Taiwan.

Moreover, encouraging democracy from the outside is difficult at best. As Larry Diamond has pointed out, "Promoting democracy does not mean exporting it."[25] Engineering foreign societies can be a dangerous business. Not every society or culture is ripe for democracy or amenable to intimate American involvement. To "demand" change of one's friends leads the United States down a path of potentially penalizing those it seeks to bolster; as the Carter administration learned in Iran, this can lead to far worse outcomes from the vantage point of human rights as well as other U.S. interests. In parts of the Arab world, rapid democratization would bring to power governments that were not only anti-American but whose commitment to democracy was tactical, a means to gain power rather than share it. What can be particularly destabilizing is pushing for elections before all aspects of a civil society are in place. This is one lesson of Algeria, where elections held early in the process of democratization brought to the fore organized forces willing to exploit but not necessarily live under greater freedom. Iran is an example of a related phenomenon: elections without democracy or even rudimentary protection of civil liberties and human rights.

It is also important to note that democracy is no panacea. In more democratic Russia, criminal elements flourish and xenophobic, nationalist elements are increasing. The former Yugoslavia is painful proof that nonliberal democracies can be extremely aggressive in treating their own people and their neighbors. Democracy cannot always compete successfully with the lure of nationalism or ensure responsible behavior by weak leaders looking for distractions from domestic travails. A more democratic China might actually be more assertive beyond its borders than currently, just as Islamic states that have introduced elements of democracy are anything but benign in their behavior. While mature democracies tend not to make war on one another, immature or developing democracies seem if anything more prone to being swayed by popular passions and the call for violence.[26]

ECONOMISM

This fourth view of American foreign policy predicates a doctrine built around the premise that the main purpose of foreign policy is to serve economic ends, principally but not exclusively the promotion of exports. Such a doctrine stems from multiple beliefs, including the view that in the post–Cold War world traditional security concerns are less pressing, domestic concerns are more salient, and the United States now needs to jettison its past willingness to look the other way when political and military allies act unfairly in economic matters, especially trade.

This, too, was an approach of the first Clinton administration, as suggested by Secretary of State Warren Christopher when he listed "economic security" as the first priority for post–Cold War foreign policy.[27] This approach reflects a sense that other traditional interests (especially those derived from strategic concerns) have receded and that we have arrived at a juncture when economic concerns can (or need to be) paramount. It also reflects a belief that what matters the most is not military force or even political control of territory but rather command of wealth and technology.[28]

The clearest manifestation of economism is an emphasis on trade issues and the promotion of exports. Such a policy can achieve some modest results, at least for a short period. In the case of Japan, arguably the most pronounced example of American attempts to boost U.S. market access, U.S. exports rose some 35 percent between 1993 and 1995, and increased approximately 80 percent in those sectors covered by bilateral trade agreements.[29] Although much of this export increase was due to changes in the yen-dollar rate and different growth rates in the two countries along with improved marketing by U.S. firms, it may also reflect (albeit to a far lesser extent) bilateral pressures that the U.S. government levied against Japan.[30]

There are several dangers with such an emphasis, however. Exports per se are not necessarily good if they require subsidies or artificially managed exchange rates to be competitive. Another risk is that a foreign policy based upon export promotion runs the risk of degenerating into a search for specified, quantifiable results— so much market share, a particular level of trade imbalance—that will only increase the role of domestic political forces (often mercantilist) in economic relationships. It is precisely this inherent impatience and demand for specific, near-term bilateral satisfaction from commercial diplomacy that characterizes contemporary results-oriented trade policy and distinguishes it from more comprehensive, long-term, multilateral approaches to expanding world trade through the adoption of common rules and procedures. Failure to meet goals tends to lead to retaliation and protectionist measures that are economically self-destructive and inconsistent with efforts to build an open trading order on a regional or global basis.

The arguments against protectionism are powerful and, in the end, decisive.[31] Protectionist policies discourage the movement of investment and economic activity to those areas of technological innovation where there is comparative advantage. (This is just one of many reasons why bilateral trade deficits are inconclusive and often misleading.) Protectionism also increases costs. Numerous studies demonstrate how a society pays many times over in higher prices for saving a small number of jobs. Protection of the American market hurts economic growth in other countries, contributing to instability and migration. Protectionist policies also invite retaliation, thereby reducing export opportunities (and jobs that tend to be higher-paying and more productive) for the United States.[32] In addition, society loses the benefit of imports, including their quality (which gives consumers greater choice) and the competition they encourage. Anyone doubting this last consideration need only ask what kind of cars Detroit would be producing today without the competition over previous decades from Japan.

On one level, the continuing appeal of protectionism is understandable, as individual workers and firms blame foreign trade practices for what is often in reality the effect of technological innovation. Indeed, free trade has been a boon to American consumers and workers. U.S. exports have increased rapidly in recent decades; the United States is the largest merchandise exporter in the world. Eleven percent of what this country produces is sold abroad. Several million jobs, many of them high-paying, would not exist were it not for the expansion of U.S. access into overseas markets.

A policy of muscular trade promotion is also of questionable desirability for larger reasons that have nothing to do with economics. It is likely to harm the overall bilateral relationship with the country in question. Such spillover or contamination could well set in motion political and military trends that over time would work against the full range of U.S. interests. A Japan or Western Europe that comes to see its relationship with the United States as being more competitive than cooperative will inevitably reorient its foreign and defense policies away from those desired by the United States; at a minimum, it would be a less automatic ally. Multilateralizing trade—and using the mechanisms for dispute resolution that form the World Trade Organization—promises to make good political as well as economic sense. The goal of American foreign policy ought to be to "de-bilateralize" trade to the extent possible. It is one of the many ironies of the first Clinton administration that it did more to bilateralize and politicize trade at the same time it helped multilateralize and depoliti-cize it through the passage of both NAFTA and the WTO.

The broader critique of economism is that a foreign policy based on economics can all too easily be overwhelmed. Instability on the Korean peninsula, in the Persian Gulf, or in south Asia can interrupt the emergence of markets and a great deal more. A foreign policy defined by economics can also be irrelevant. As *New York Times* columnist Thomas Friedman has written, "The Serbs are not shelling Sarajevo in a mad quest for more jobs; Israelis and Palestinians are not still killing each other because of differing interpretations of the GATT agreement."[33] Amid war or revolution, the primacy of economics will come to a sudden end; "geo-economics" will find itself taking a back seat to geopolitics. Similarly, the desire to sell for economic reasons can easily come into conflict with the need to penalize or isolate a country for political or strategic purposes. The world of deregulation remains too dangerous for the United States to view it largely much less exclusively through an economic lens.

HUMANITARIANISM

The humanitarian approach is embraced by people who tend to see the world less in terms of nation-states than as peoples. They tend to view threats less in terms of aggression than chaos. Foreign policy humanitarians focus on such concerns—the alleviation of poverty, disease, hunger, overpopulation, the environment, and so on—because they are important in their own right and because these problems can lead to more traditional conflicts if their consequences go untended.[34]

Humanitarianism is another competing element of Clinton foreign policy. Characteristic is the statement by Under Secretary of State Timothy Wirth: "Crisis prevention and the challenge of sustainable development are among the greatest challenges for the remainder of this and into the next century. It is time to retool our approach to national security."[35] Also representative are the words of Clinton administration Agency for International Development

(AID) Director J. Brian Atwood: "Disintegrating societies and failed states with their civil conflicts and destabilizing refugee flows have emerged as the greatest menace to global stability."[36]

The problem with the humanitarian view is not so much its accuracy—overpopulation, food and water shortages, and environmental degradation are all real problems certain to grow worse over time—as its adequacy. Humanitarianism underestimates other concerns and threats that are more immediate and important and that need to inform any foreign policy. It is at most a supplementary world view, not an independent one.[37] Moreover, many of the problems that animate humanitarianism are extremely difficult to fix. At the same time, these basic social and developmental problems do not normally threaten directly U.S. national interests. It is thus difficult to rally domestic support for expensive efforts to address humanitarian problems abroad, especially when many of the same socioeconomic problems are to be found in this country. As is true for Wilsonianism, addressing humanitarian concerns can contribute to a foreign policy doctrine, not define one.

REALISM

The essence of the realist perspective is its focus on nation-states as the principal actors in the world and on the maintenance of order *between* rather than *within* states. Realists emphasize balance-of-power considerations—a basic form of international regulation—when it comes to the national interest. Alliances among like-minded governments are a favored vehicle for promoting these interests. Realists are sensitive to the prerequisites of sovereignty, fearing that its weakening will only increase the threat or use of military force in international relations. Those who hold this view are mindful of the continuing threats posed by regional military powers and the potential strategic challenges of Russia or China. Realists are much less concerned with the internal character of foreign societies and with such matters as human rights, democracy and humanitarian welfare, all of which they would describe as preferences rather than interests. Realists do, however, support liberal trade and multilateral (instead of unilateral) remedies on the grounds that they, too, reinforce orderly interstate relations.[38]

The strength of the realist approach is that it highlights existing and potential threats to major U.S. interests that, if they were to materialize, could overwhelm all other policy concerns. Realists also correctly understand that in most situations states continue to be the most powerful units on the global chessboard and that dealing with classical forms of interstate aggression is what U.S. military forces do best. Realism was very much the orientation of both the Nixon and Bush foreign policies.

The principal weakness of realism is that it provides no guidelines (other than to stand aloof) for dealing with important if less than vital economic, political, and humanitarian problems within states, arguably the potential source of most post–Cold War instability. Realism offers little help in determining whether and, if so, how to deal with such problems as Somalia, the former Yugoslavia, Rwanda, Haiti, even post–Cold War Cuba. Such problems can be important even if they do not touch directly on the United States. Not all interests need be vital to be worthy of American attention or protection.

Realism suffers as well from its lack of popular appeal. An emphasis on international order and stability does not impart much purpose to foreign policy. The promotion of order, however important and necessary, is not enough. It cannot engage the broader American public and Congress, who want and often require a larger purpose as a prerequisite for supporting foreign policy.[39] The result is that a narrow realism cannot be sustained by a country and a people that are uncomfortable with realpolitik and pride themselves on their morality and their exceptionalism.

A DOCTRINE OF REGULATION

What should be done? Which of these six doctrines—hegemony, isolationism, democracy promotion, economism, humanitarianism, or realism—makes the most sense for the United States to adopt in a deregulated world? The short answer is none of them individually, but rather several of them combined.

The ideal doctrine resembles realism the most. The principal focus of American foreign policy should be on interstate relations and the external conduct of states—discouraging classic aggression, acquisition of weapons of mass destruction by rogue states, protectionism, state support for terrorism, illegal entry. These matters have the greatest potential to affect the most important U.S. interests most deeply. As Joseph Nye has written, "Political order [between states] is not sufficient to explain economic prosperity, but it is necessary. Analysts who ignore the importance of political order are like people who forget the importance of the oxygen they breathe."[40] Nye's insight applies equally to those who argue that human rights or broad humanitarian concerns or exports ought to dominate foreign policy.

The focus on interstate concerns, however, should be dominant rather than exclusive. Considerations of "justice"—democracy, human rights, human welfare—would, though, ordinarily be of a lower priority. So, too, would be economic aims. The reasoning here is simple. Order is the more basic concern. One can have order without justice but not the other way around. Similarly, one cannot have trade without stability and peace.

The best term for such a policy amalgam is "regulation." Under this doctrine, the United States would act, whenever possible with others but alone when necessary and feasible, to shape the behavior and, in some cases, capabilities of governments and other actors so that they are less likely or able to act aggressively either beyond their borders or toward their own citizens and more likely to conduct trade and other economic relations according to agreed norms and procedures.

In a fully regulated world, democratic governments and other actors would comport themselves according to a set of universal norms reflecting the rule of law. Military force would not be used by governments in their relations with one another; no state would harbor or in any way support terrorists. Within states, there would be clear respect for human rights. Trade disputes would be decided under the WTO or some other body, while governments would agree to guidelines that prevent or limit practices that would affect the environment.

If history is any guide, such a perfect world is not about to emerge—certainly not on its own. In the imperfect geopolitical marketplace, no invisible hand ensures maximum "efficiency." The aim of American foreign policy is to work with other like-minded actors to "improve" the marketplace, to increase compliance with basic norms, by choice if possible, by necessity, i.e., coercion, if need be. At its core, regulation is an imperial doctrine in that it seeks to promote a set of standards we endorse, something not to be confused with imperialism, which is a foreign policy of exploitation.

As a result, relations *between* states should normally take precedence over conditions *within* states, as the former is the more likely to directly affect our interests as opposed to our preferences. In addition, threats posed to states by other states or other externally based or supported actors tend to be more amenable to being fixed or at least ameliorated by available policy tools. In instances where a state's foreign policy is of little consequence, the United States has the luxury of focusing its policy on the country's internal practices. This will lead to charges of inconsistency, but inconsistency is the price of priorities. It is better for the United States to be selective in the priority it accords to promoting democracy, human rights, and market reforms than either to make them the priority for foreign policy everywhere, something we cannot afford given our other interests, or nowhere, something that would unnecessarily limit our potential to be a positive force. Irving Kristol makes this point with characteristic directness: "[N]ot only does our foreign policy have a double standard with regard to what is now called 'human rights,' but we have a triple and quadruple standard as well. Indeed, we have as many standards as circumstances require—which is as it should be."[41]

Does regulation qualify as a doctrine? By definition, doctrines must not only indicate a sense of interests (and priorities) but also a guide to intentions. It must offer instruction to policymakers as well as to Congress, the American public, and allies and adversaries alike.[42] The Truman Doctrine did just that, in indicating that the United States opposed the spread of Soviet power and influence and was prepared to act against it. So, too, did other lesser doctrines announced by Jimmy Carter (to resist challenges to U.S. interests in the oil-producing Persian Gulf) and Ronald Reagan (in making clear U.S. readiness to assist movements opposed to existing Communist or pro-Soviet regimes).

As a doctrine, regulation is certainly not as developed in all its potential applications as was containment. But containment did not offer all that much guidance either when first articulated. More important, even after several decades, reasonable and informed people still argued over just what containment called for. The idea that a foreign policy doctrine makes decisions about particular foreign policies easy or obvious is absurd; a degree of judgment and case-by-case analysis are as necessary as ever. Were it otherwise, we never would have experienced prolonged and intense debates over Korea, Vietnam, China, Euromissiles, and Central America, to name just a few.[43]

What would regulation entail in practice? It calls for a continued orientation of U.S. national security toward the Persian Gulf, the Asia-Pacific, and Europe. The United States has a vital interest in a favorable balance of power in these three regions of great economic and military resources. This does not mean it can or should be our goal (as urged by advocates of American hegemony) to prevent the emergence of any challenge to such a balance. This would be impossible in some instances or commit us to an endless series of preventive attacks in others. Rather, we must act to maintain acceptable balances through countering or offsetting any imbalance as it occurs, be it from a local state or an emerging great power. This interest clearly places a premium on stemming the proliferation of weapons of mass destruction to rogue elements, as no other change has the potential to affect the calculations of balance so quickly.

As has been pointed out, however, regulation transcends traditional realism. There are opportunities to promote democracy or human rights, just as there are obligations to protect peoples (especially victims of genocide) that cannot in good conscience be ignored. Regulation thus takes elements of both Wilsonianism and humanitarianism and grafts them on to realism to produce a broader synthesis. At the same time, regulation tends to reject rather than borrow from other would-be doctrines on grounds that neo-isolationism is unwise, hegemony unworkable, and economism both too narrow and flawed.

Some might argue that there is no need for such a choice among priorities. For example, the United States has a clear interest in promoting market reforms wherever possible but especially in Russia, China, and India—not only for economic reasons but as the best way to encourage the emergence of pluralism at home and peaceful behavior abroad. Similarly, the United States supports the growth of democracy in these countries. In principle, any foreign policy should seek to foster order and justice alike, as what is good for the latter also proves to be conducive to the former.

But at some point a foreign policy must act on priorities. Action—be it a sanction or military intervention or simply a diplomatic demarche—on behalf of one concern could jeopardize others. China is the perfect case. The United States has multiple interests, including deterring any Chinese use of force against Taiwan, expanding American exports, discouraging Chinese provision of nuclear technology to Pakistan or any other state, eliciting diplomatic assistance vis-à-vis North Korea and in the U.N. Security Council more generally, fostering democracy and market reform, and encouraging respect for human rights and sound environmental policy. All can be pursued, but not equally. A doctrine of regulation would emphasize most China's ability to affect regional or even global stability—even at the price of losing out to European exporters or not introducing sanctions over human rights violations.

Regulation provides similar yardsticks for other situations where multiple concerns are at stake. U.S. policy toward Russia, for example, needs to be dominated by concerns over the security of nuclear weapons and materials and working with Russia to promote stability in Europe and elsewhere. Attempts to foster democracy and market reform should be secondary, in part because other interests cannot be postponed, in part because our leverage is likely to be greater in affecting Russia's external behavior than its social and political order.

With Japan, continuing and where possible expanding political and military cooperation would take precedence over promoting exports, an interest that would be dealt with through multilateral means to the extent possible. (The April 1996 U.S.–Japan Communiqué was thus a welcome corrective. Similarly, the June 1996 decision to use the WTO rather than U.S. law to press Kodak's case against Japan and Fuji was a step in the right direction.) A good U.S.–Japan relationship is essential if the United States is to be in a position to cope with military developments on the Korean peninsula and manage the challenge posed by an increasingly powerful China.

U.S. policy toward the Middle East and the Persian Gulf should be informed more by efforts to stem unconventional weapons proliferation and threats to regional balance than by a desire to encourage democratic reform. This is because of the pressing vital interest of maintaining access to oil, the immediacy of the threats, and the difficulty of promoting democracy in traditional societies. This is not to suggest that nothing be done on the latter score—the United States should quietly support the gradual emergence of civil society, representative institutions, market reforms, and control of corruption—but these are difficult, long-term enterprises.

In Africa and Latin America, where U.S. strategic interests are modest for the most part, regulation would direct U.S. policy to promote market reform and democracy. This emphasis would apply even to Cuba, no longer a strategic threat in the wake of the Cold War and the demise of its military ties to Moscow.

Together, the determination of a paradigm and a doctrine—in this case, deregulation and regulation—provide a great deal of direction. But such determinations are not the end of the policy process. Still to be decided are questions relating to how to go about the task of implementing the doctrine. This is in part a matter of form. What degree of unilateralism is called for, as opposed to what degree and kind of multilateralism? It is also a matter of tools. How much military force as opposed to how much diplomacy is best? And what ground rules should shape the application of these and other policy instruments? These questions form the core of the next two chapters.

NOTES

1. For a useful attempt to weigh U.S. interests, see *America's National Interests: A Report from the Commission on America's National Interests* (Washington, D.C.: Commission on America's National Interests, 1996).
2. Other analysts have put forth different templates for deconstructing the post–Cold War policy debate. See, for example, Alexander Nacht, "U.S. Foreign Policy Strategies," *Washington Quarterly* 18, no. 3 (Summer 1995), 1195–1210, and Barry Posen and Andrew L. Ross, "Competing Visions for U.S. Grand Strategy," *International Security* 21, no. 3 (Winter 1996/97), 5–53.
3. Excerpts of the Department of Defense's February 18 Draft Defense Planning Guidance were printed in the *New York Times*, March 8, 1992, A14.
4. Irving Kristol, "Defining Our National Interest," *National Interest*, no. 21 (Fall 1990), 23.
5. William Kristol and Robert Kagan, "Toward a Neo-Reaganite Foreign Policy," *Foreign Affairs* 75, no. 4 (July/August, 1996), 23.
6. Charles Krauthammer, "What's Wrong with the 'Pentagon Paper'?" *Washington Post*, March 13, 1992, A25, and "The Unipolar Moment," *Foreign Affairs* 70, no. 1 (1990–1991), 32.
7. For additional explications and rationales for unipolarity or primacy, see Zalmay Khalilzad, "Losing the Moment? The United States and the World After the Cold War," *Washington Quarterly* 18, no. 2 (Spring 1995), 87–107, and Francis Fukuyama, "The Beginning of Foreign Policy," *New Republic* (August 17 & 24, 1992), 24–32. Sample criticisms include Christopher Layne, "The Unipolar Illusion: Why New Great Powers Will Rise," *International Security* 17, no. 14 (Spring 1993), 5–51, and Robert Jervis, "International Primacy: Is the Game Worth the Candle?" *International Security* 17, no. 4 (Spring 1993), 52–67.
8. Kenneth N. Waltz, "The Emerging Structure of International Politics," *International Security* 18, no. 2 (Fall 1993), 66.
9. Kristol and Kagan, "Toward a Neo-Reaganite Foreign Policy," *Foreign Affairs* 75, no. 4 (July/August, 1996), 23.
10. China and Russia cited "hegemonism" along with "power politics and repeated imposition of pressures on other countries" as constituting threats to international tranquility when they met in Shanghai in late April 1996.
11. Examples of minimalist thinking include Earl C. Ravenal, "The Case for Adjustment," *Foreign Policy*, no. 81 (Winter 1990–91), 3–19; Ted Galen Carpenter, "The New World Disorder," *Foreign Policy*, no. 84 (Fall 1991), 24–39; Christopher Layne and Benjamin Schwartz, "American Hegemony—Without an Enemy," *Foreign Policy*, no. 92 (Fall 1993), 5–23; William R.

Hawkins, "Isolationism, Properly Understood," *National Interest*, no. 24 (Summer 1991), 61–66; and Patrick J. Buchanan, "America First—and Second, and Third," *National Interest*, no. 19 (Spring 1990), 77–82.

12. Jonathan Clarke, "The Conceptual Poverty of U.S. Foreign Policy," *Atlantic Monthly* (September 1993), 65. Such perspectives are not confined to those on the political "left"; also see Robert D. Novak, "A Search for New Enemies," *Washington Post*, August 28, 1995, A23.

13. Ronald Steel, "Beware the Superpower Syndrome," *New York Times*, April 25, 1994, A15. For a more complete sense of Steel's views, see his *Temptations of a Superpower* (Cambridge, Mass.: Harvard University Press, 1995).

14. Alan Tonelson, "Clinton's World: The Realities of America's Post–Cold War Foreign Policy," in Eugene R. Wittkopf (ed.), *The Future of American Foreign Policy*, 2nd ed. (New York: St. Martin's, 1994), 49.

15. William G. Hyland, "Downgrade Foreign Policy," *New York Times*, May 20, 1991, A15. For similar preferences, see Jonathan Clarke and James Clad, *After the Crusade: American Foreign Policy for the Post–Superpower Age* (Lanham, Md.: Madison Books, 1995).

16. Paul Kennedy, *The Rise and Fall of the Great Powers: Economic Change and Military Conflict from 1500 to 2000* (New York: Random House, 1987). A strong counterweight to Kennedy's perspective can be found in Joseph S. Nye Jr., *Bound to Lead: The Changing Nature of American Power* (New York: Basic Books, 1990). For an assessment of Kennedy and his critics, see Charles A. Kupchan, "Empire, Military Power, and Economic Decline," *International Security* 13, no. 4 (Spring 1989), 36–53.

17. Daniel Williams and John M. Goshko, "Reduced U.S. World Role Outlined but Soon Altered," *Washington Post*, May 26, 1993, A1, A24.

18. For a similar line of argumentation, see Joshua Muravchik, "Affording Foreign Policy," *Foreign Affairs* 75, no. 2 (March/April 1996), 8–13.

19. This is in addition to the problems faced by communities and individuals who lose jobs because of plant and base closings. See *The Economic Effects of Reduced Defense Spending* (Washington, D.C.: CBO, 1992).

20. See, for example, Robert D. Hormats, "The Roots of American Power," *Foreign Affairs* 70, no. 3 (Summer 1991), 132–149.

21. There is an enormous literature on this subject. See, among others, Bruce Russett, *Grasping the Democratic Peace: Principles for a Post–Cold War World* (Princeton, N.J.: Princeton University Press, 1993); Tony Smith, *America's Mission: The United States and the Worldwide Struggle for Democracy in the Twentieth Century* (Princeton, N.J.: Princeton University Press, 1994); and Joshua Muravchik, *Exporting Democracy: Fulfilling America's Destiny* (Washington, D.C.: American Enterprise Institute, 1991).

22. Lake's address of September 21, 1993, is reprinted in *U.S. Department of State Dispatch* 4, no. 39 (September 27, 1993), 658–64. Also see Strobe Talbott, "Democracy and the National Interest," *Foreign Affairs* 75, no. 6 (November/December 1996), 47–63.

23. See, for example, Robert Kagan, "A Retreat From Power?" *Commentary* 100, no. 1 (July 1995), 19–25; Joshua A. Muravchik, *The Imperative of American Leadership: A Challenge to Neo-Isolationism* (Washington, D.C.:

AEI, 1996) and Michael A. Ledeen, *Freedom Betrayed: How America Led a Global Revolution, Won the Cold War, and Walked Away* (Washington, D.C.: AEI, 1996).

24. For a critique of the first Clinton administration in this realm, see Thomas Carothers, "Democracy Promotion Under Clinton," *Washington Quarterly* 18, no. 4 (Autumn 1995), 13–25.

25. Larry Diamond, "Promoting Democracy," *Foreign Policy*, no. 87 (Summer 1992), 27.

26. This same conclusion is reached by Edward D. Mansfield and Jack Snyder, "Democratization and War," *Foreign Affairs* 74, no. 3 (May–June, 1995), 79–97. Also see William R. Thompson, "Democracy and Peace: Putting the Cart Before the Horse?" *International Organization* 50, no. 1 (Winter 1996), 141–174, and Samuel P. Huntington, "Democracy for the Long Haul," *Journal of Democracy* 7, no. 2 (April 1996), 3–13.

27. See Warren Christopher, "The Strategic Priorities of American Foreign Policy," statement on November 4, 1993 before the Senate Foreign Relations Committee, reprinted in *U.S. Department of State Dispatch* 4, no. 47 (November 22, 1993), 797–802.

28. See, for example, C. Fred Bergsten, "The Primacy of Economics," *Foreign Policy*, no. 87 (Summer 1992), 3–24, and Susan Strange, "The Name of the Game," in Nicholas X. Rizopoulos (ed.), *Sea-Changes: American Foreign Policy in a World Transformed* (New York: Council on Foreign Relations, 1990), 238–73.

29. See *Economic Report of the President* (Washington, D.C.: U.S. Government Printing Office, 1996), 245–47.

30. For a discussion of these considerations, see Franklin L. Lavin, "Boosting Export Figures, Not Exports," *Wall Street Journal*, June 6, 1996, A14, as well as the *Economic Report of the President* cited above.

31. See, for example, *Economic Report of the President* (Washington, D.C.: U.S. Government Printing Office, 1996), 225–60; Roger C. Altman, "Buchanan: Backward on Trade," *Washington Post*, March 5, 1996, A15; Paul Krugman, "Free Trade and Protectionism," in Wittkopf (ed.), *The Future of American Foreign Policy*, 337–44; and Jagdish N. Bhagwati, *Protectionism* (Cambridge, Mass.: MIT Press, 1988).

32. See J. David Richardson and Karin Rindal, *Why Exports Matter: More!* (Washington, D.C.: Institute for International Economics and the Manufacturing Institute, 1996).

33. Thomas L. Friedman, "Is a Diplomacy of Dollars Really Enough?" *New York Times*, December 12, 1993, E5.

34. For background, see Jessica Tuchman Mathews, "Redefining Security," *Foreign Affairs* 68, no. 2 (Spring 1989), 162–77.

35. Address by Timothy Wirth to National Press Club, July 12, 1994.

36. J. Brian Atwood, "Suddenly, Chaos," *Washington Post*, July 31, 1994, C9.

37. For a similar critique, see Jeremy D. Rosner, "Is Chaos America's Real Enemy?" *Washington Post*, August 14, 1994, C1–2.

38. For insight into realist thinking, see Henry Kissinger, "What Kind of New World Order?" *Washington Post*, December 3, 1991, A21; Peter W. Rod-

man, "Points of Order," *National Review* (May 1, 1995), 36–42, 88; and Fareed Zakaria, "Realism Reconsidered," *National Interest*, no. 30 (Winter 1992/93), 21–32.

39. For a critique of realism along these lines, see George Weigel, "On the Road to Isolationism," *Commentary* (January 1992), 36–42.

40. Joseph S. Nye, Jr., "The Case for Deep Engagement," *Foreign Affairs* 74, no. 4 (July–August, 1995), 91.

41. Irving Kristol, "Defining Our National Interest," *National Interest*, no. 21 (Fall 1990), 24.

42. On determining the requirements of a doctrine, I benefited from an unpublished paper by Vincent A. Auger of Hamilton College.

43. Charles Krauthammer makes just this point in a column that takes to task those who justify current foreign policy difficulties on the grounds that it was so much easier during the Cold War. See his "The Greatest Cold War Myth of All," *Time* (November 29, 1993), 86.

Chapter 4

Foreign Policy by Posse

A doctrine of regulation will not simply implement itself, any more than declaring containment to be America's purpose during the Cold War made it happen. What is required is a viable approach to the world, a mechanism for translating doctrine into policy or, more precisely, policies.

During the Cold War, the principal vehicle for American foreign policy was a network of alliances in which the United States worked closely with selected states who shared a similar perception of the Soviet Union and communism. The dependence on alliances is understandable, as they provide a mechanism for pooling resources and joining forces with like-minded states against common threats. Alliances also provide a mechanism for deterrence and for preparing defensive (or offensive) actions, thereby generating leverage and enabling a country to accomplish more than it could if forced to act on its own.

During the Cold War, the most important of these alliances was the North Atlantic Treaty Organization (NATO), a body that came to include 16 countries on both sides of the Atlantic pledged to responding collectively if any was attacked from without. These countries not only shared a commitment to democracy but were able and willing to contribute to the common defense against a common threat.

There was no parallel to NATO in other regions, a reflection of differences in geography and politics alike. In the Asia–Pacific area, for example, a common physical front was lacking. More important, different countries had different perceptions of what threat mattered the most. Some of these countries were democracies, others were authoritarian. As a result, the United States forged individual defense alliances with Japan, the Republic of Korea (South Korea), Australia, and New Zealand, and with the Southeast Asia Treaty Organization (SEATO) countries—Australia, Great Britain, France, New Zealand, Pakistan, the Philippines, and Thailand—as well as Cambodia, Laos, and South Vietnam under a special protocol. SEATO, never terribly effective, dissolved formally in 1977, although the United States did retain treaty ties to several of its former members.

An attempt in the mid–1950s to build an alliance structure in the Persian Gulf and Middle East, the so-called Central Treaty Organization (CENTO), unraveled soon after its creation. The reason is both simple and significant. For any alliance to work, it must be based on a shared purpose and a common sense of threat. CENTO met neither test. For the United States, the threat was communism and Soviet expansionism. For the Arab states of the area, the threat tended to be Israel, while for Pakistan it was India. The United States did forge an increasingly intimate relationship with Israel, although even this tie fell short of a formal alliance.

In Latin America, any effort to build meaningful alliances would have run aground because for many countries of the hemisphere, the United States constituted the principal threat to their independence. The Rio Treaty, the principal security arrangement linking the United States to countries of the Western Hemisphere, was more a declaratory framework than a working alliance. No attempt was made to build an alliance structure in Africa: this was less a decision than a reflection of the relative absence of interests and threats. Any such effort would have foundered on a lack of local capability and the absence of consensus over what constituted the enemy. The result was that in Latin America and Africa, regional security became based on largely ineffectual regional organizations (the Organization of American States and the Organization of African Unity, respectively) and sometimes effective U.S. activism.

The question arises whether alliances in general, and whether these alliances in particular, will and should continue to play so central a role in American foreign policy. If not, what should take their place?

There is no single answer to such questions. Again, there are choices to be made. Some analysts advocate maintaining alliances—and in some cases the same ones—as the foundation for U.S. foreign policy. A second approach largely eschews alliances in favor of a more unilateral approach by the United States. A third approach could not be more different: establishing a new emphasis on international institutions as the principal means to promote foreign policy aims in a deregulated world. A fourth approach would have the United States forge temporary coalitions of states and others able and willing to participate in the endeavor of the moment.

These four approaches are not mutually exclusive. No foreign policy could fit entirely into one category and ignore the others. Yet, there are real differences in emphasis with real consequences. The debate over this country's approach to the world is no less important or intense than the debate over doctrine and priorities. Indeed, the choice of doctrine becomes largely academic if it is not accompanied by an effective foreign policy to back it up.

ALLIANCES

The traditional, organizational approach that so often characterized American foreign policy over the past half-century was exemplified by NATO. NATO was possible because the international situation was, for all its potential dangers, essentially stable. Standing alliances require predictability as regards the source of problems and clarity as regards those friends and allies who can be counted upon to act against them. Time is needed to consider scenarios and to prepare plans and capabilities for addressing them. NATO was made possible by the threat of a Soviet/Warsaw Pact attack on Western Europe and the collective readiness of the United States, Canada and NATO's 14 European members to resist aggression in that place.

NATO was a highly effective Cold War instrument that deserves considerable credit for maintaining peace in Europe and determining the Cold War's outcome. Still, as useful as this institution was, it had its limits. NATO was unable to force governments to do much of anything. Like any true alliance, it was an association of sovereign members. France could not be compelled to remain in NATO's united military command. Several governments balked at supporting the deployment of intermediate-range missiles in Western Europe. Member states regularly fell short of goals set for their military contributions.

Moreover, NATO tended not to deal well with scenarios that diverged from those that led to its creation. The need for consensus and voluntary adherence to collective decisions often became a rationale for inaction. NATO was helpless to contend with problems between its members—the friction between Greece and Turkey over Cyprus comes to mind. NATO also could do little to solve problems inside one of its members or meet challenges that might affect most or even all its members but fell outside the area covered by its charter.

What about the future? What could and should NATO do in the age of deregulation? In principle, any alliance has four choices when confronted by a fundamental change in circumstances. It can try to do familiar things in new places. NATO, for example, could in principle seek to become central to protecting Western interests outside Europe. Second, an alliance can try to do new things in familiar places. NATO could take on new missions in Europe, possibly growing in the process. Third, NATO could dissolve itself. Fourth, NATO could find a way to continue doing what it does but at a lower level of effort more commensurate with the reduced threat it faces. Any but the third option could be carried out by the current 16-member NATO or by a larger organization.[1]

Could NATO become even more important in the deregulated world, essentially exchanging its mission of deterring Soviet invasion of Europe for one of regional or even global peacemaking and defense? One set of analysts argues just this, claiming that "NATO must go out of area or it will go out of business."[2] After all, NATO remains a unique association of militarily capable states with a highly professional staff, attributes that enable the alliance to undertake demanding military operations, including in the Persian Gulf. Moreover, France is now reintegrating itself with NATO's military arm, and new members may be added to the alliance. In short, could NATO become an alliance that regulates a deregulated world?[3]

The short answer is no. NATO's military capabilities are much reduced and getting smaller as members adjust to the post–Cold War environment, including the demise of the Warsaw Pact and the weakening of Russia. In addition, there is barely enough political will and consensus to deal with the Bosnian contingency, much less the threats posed by Iran and Iraq. Moreover, to get NATO members to devote more resources to defense would probably require the reemergence of a clear Russian threat. But dealing with such a challenge would absorb any new NATO strength, leaving little or nothing for the rest of the world or for other contingencies within Europe. The United States would be wiser to tap individually those NATO members able and willing to assist in particular situations, such as France and Great Britain in a future Gulf conflict, and draw on organizational assets such as communications and intelligence links, rather than deal with the organization itself.

At least two missions in Europe might offer a new rationale for NATO. Helping to secure the orientation of former Warsaw Pact states is one. By expanding to take in Poland, Hungary, the Czech Republic, and potentially others, NATO could provide a reassuring anchor for these newly democratic and Western-oriented countries. In addition, an enlarged NATO would also be a hedge against renewed Russian aggression.

There are strong arguments against expansion, however. Expansion (or enlargement) would increase the defense demands on

NATO and the United States, cause problems for Western relations with Russia, and exacerbate the insecurity of countries (including the Baltic states and Ukraine) that remain outside the NATO umbrella. In addition, the principal advantage of enlargement—securing democracy and Western orientation—could be accomplished at least in part through other institutions, for example, expansion of the European Union (EU). Enlargement that brought in too many states would dilute NATO's character and undermine the credibility of the core alliance commitment by which every member pledges to come to the defense of any member that is attacked.

On balance, the debate over NATO enlargement is an unfortunate and unnecessary one. The Clinton administration created a perfectly adequate vehicle—the Partnership for Peace—that provided a menu of potential political and military links to former Warsaw Pact states without raising many of the drawbacks of formal NATO enlargement. But once the option of inclusion in NATO was put on the table, the Partnership for Peace was seen as lacking by central Europeans—just as the option of NATO enlargement became more menacing to many Russians. Still, now that the promise of NATO enlargement exists, an American failure to follow through would create fundamental questions about U.S. reliability and steadfastness while appearing to reward Russian hostility. The best course at this point would be to offer alliance membership to a minimum number of states, add substance to the Partnership for Peace for those left out, and proceed with enlargement in a manner that takes legitimate Russian concerns into account, including indicating that we have no intention of stationing outside forces or nuclear weapons in the territory of any new member. Arms control arrangements created to maintain stability between NATO and the Warsaw Pact should be revised to reflect new political and military realities in Europe. NATO should also negotiate an agreement with the Russians that offers an opportunity to participate in selected NATO operations and gives them a voice but not a veto (or membership) in NATO counsels. More important for our purposes here, however, it is doubtful that expansion alone—on these or any other terms—offers enough of a *military* mission to justify the alliance's continuation.[4]

Peacemaking and peacekeeping in Europe is an example of finding a new role in familiar territory. The former Yugoslavia illustrates what NATO can do. Once consensus was reached to act in mid-1995, NATO proved to be effective, first with coercive air attacks and then with a ground presence that made a cease-fire possible and potentially lasting. But at closer examination, this was not so much NATO as the United States, France, and Great Britain acting collectively (as a combined joint task force or CJTF) using NATO planning and support staff. As Josef Joffe has correctly pointed out, "It was an American-led effort to make parts of NATO a party to the war."[5] Just as important, NATO would be unlikely to be able to do more of the same should, say, a crisis break out elsewhere in the Balkans, especially if it involved Greece and/or Turkey.

What about going out of business? The core mission—protecting members against a hostile external threat—is essentially in mothballs so long as Russia's conventional military forces remain weak and its leadership less than hostile toward the United States and Europe. The demise of the Soviet threat makes NATO something of a vestigial organization. If it did not already exist, it would be impossible to create it.[6]

But NATO does already exist, and it continues to tie the United States to Europe, thereby constituting a valuable bulwark against American isolationism and European parochialism. NATO and the transatlantic tie help provide reassurance and a foreign policy framework for an increasingly powerful Germany. NATO also provides a central organization from which to draw forces and staff elements for operations in and around Europe. NATO enlargement does offer concrete benefits to new members. Most of all, NATO provides insurance against uncertainty in the former Soviet Union. The result is that the United States benefits from a functioning NATO that is oriented toward Europe, able to contend with modest levels of internal strife and contribute to selective efforts beyond Europe, and maintain itself intact as a hedge against what may evolve in the former Soviet Union. There is thus a role for it in a deregulated world—even if that role is different and less central than was the case before.

What about this country's other alliances? The U.S.-South Korean tie is robust but only for a single contingency: to deter and if need be defend against the threat from the North. The relationship would need to be modified significantly if the peninsula came to be reunified in the aftermath of the North's collapse or its conquest by the United States and the South—a likely result of any war initiated by the North. But even in that context there would still be utility in maintaining a close U.S.-Korean relationship and an American military presence on the peninsula to discourage a Korean nuclear weapons program, to help avoid a reemergence of Korean-Japanese tensions, and to avoid "singularizing" Japan as the only country in the area still hosting a large number of American forces. Similar arguments apply to maintaining and even expanding security ties with Australia and New Zealand.

The U.S.-Japanese alliance is something else again. Despite the end of the Cold War, this alliance continues to provide a useful umbrella for Japan's participation in the world, making it less necessary for Japan to become self-reliant for its own defense and thus avoiding a chain of events that could prove costly and destabilizing in the region. In this way, the American alliance with Japan performs a function similar to that with Germany.

This alliance could have a new lease on life should war break out on the Korean peninsula. The joint declaration that was signed during President Clinton's April 1996 visit to Japan represented movement in the direction of closer cooperation in dealing with regional contingencies.[7] The goal should be a greater but still constrained Japanese military role so as not to alarm Japan's neighbors and trigger regional realignments—and closer cooperation to help discourage a Chinese or Russian threat from emerging or to help manage it if it does.

In the Persian Gulf, the scene of the first major war of the age of deregulation, there is no prospect for an alliance in the traditional sense. The local states that the United States would want to defend from attack would be unwilling (for fear of alienating powerful anti-Western domestic constituencies) to enter into such a bond. Moreover, they would have little to contribute militarily beyond access to their territory and support. Just as important, such states are potentially vulnerable to internal instability, something a traditional alliance presence cannot manage and might actually exacerbate. Lesser forms of defense collaboration are all that can be counted on.

Elsewhere, only Israel appears as a possibility for an alliance relationship with the United States. (Other countries, such as India, are candidates for much closer strategic relationships but not alliances.) Such an arrangement with Israel would build upon the already deep ties and cooperation between the two countries. A formal commitment from the United States could buttress peace prospects by enhancing Israeli confidence and by further signaling to radical forces in the region that Israel is there to stay. The drawbacks, however, argue against formalizing this relationship. Integrating Israel into U.S. strategy for the region (and overcoming Arab problems with such close U.S. cooperation with Israel) could raise more problems than it would solve. So, too, could arrangements whereby there is allowance for Israel to act when it deems necessary but when the United States wishes it would not.

The overall conclusion of this survey is that alliances can contribute to but by themselves will not be able to furnish a mechanism for implementing a doctrine of regulation. Groups of countries that once shared a common purpose now no longer do or do so only in increasingly less common circumstances. Alliances require a large degree of predictability as regards threat and a large degree of commonality as regards priorities and what countries are willing to do on their behalf. Such agreement must exist long before the situation actually arises so the alliance can be formed and so capacities can be developed. But precisely those characteristics tend to be lacking in the age of deregulation.

UNILATERALISM

Unilateralism is an approach to U.S. involvement in the world that minimizes and wherever possible excludes the participation of other governments and organizations. Unilateralists are uncomfortable with the compromises necessary for the smooth functioning of alliances, and they oppose any transfer of substantial authority to international organizations. The 1989 U.S. invasion of Panama was a unilateral exercise, as for all intents and purposes were the interventions in Grenada and Haiti (at least in its initial phase and despite a U.N. blessing). Also essentially unilateral were the limited military strikes carried out by U.S. forces against Iraq in the aftermath of the attempt on the life of former President George Bush and then again in September 1996 after some 40,000 Iraqi forces supported one Kurdish faction against another. Sanctions against Cuba are increasingly a unilateral endeavor, as are most aspects of the latest sanctions against Iran and Libya. The United States broke ranks over NATO's enforcement of the Bosnian arms embargo and many in Congress threatened to push this country to abrogate the embargo unilaterally. At the same time, and despite membership in the World Trade Organization, the Clinton administration prepared sanctions against Japan in reaction to restraints affecting the marketing of American-made automobiles and parts in Japan. The administration also threatened sanctions against others (including China, Indonesia, India, and France) in disputes over market access.

The list could go on and no doubt will. Explaining why acting alone is as popular as it is is not all that hard, given the obvious advantages. It is much easier to act without having to gain the consent of others. No compromise is necessary; Congress in particular seems attracted to supporting "pure" positions. Unilateralism maximizes speed and freedom of decision making and implementation, including the elimination of problems of military interoperability with others. It also is easier to keep secrets.

Moreover, two features of the post–Cold War international environment—less automatic resistance from great-power adversaries and less dependable assistance from erstwhile allies—also reinforce the temptation and at times the necessity of acting alone. Unilateralism can be the best option for acting when narrow interests are at stake and where the involvement of others is not necessary logistically or is deemed undesirable, lest surprise be sacrificed or a friend embarrassed. Both Panama and Grenada fit this bill. Retaliating against state sponsorship of terror, for example, the

U.S. strikes against Iraq after the failed attempt on the life of former President Bush, is best done by the United States acting alone. In this latter circumstance, new technologies, such as ship-launched cruise missiles, enable the United States to strike a limited set of targets with little or no third-country involvement.

A unilateral approach, however, has considerable problems. It reinforces an activism that can easily be emulated and abused by others. Unilateral military action in the Western Hemisphere risks leading others to believe they can act similarly in what they regard as their sphere of influence. In addition, American unilateralism will inevitably produce resistance if not backlash. An à la carte approach to alliances and other international arrangements—the sort of behavior manifested by the United States in its November 1994 decision to cease participating in the enforcement of the Bosnian arms embargo or by unilateral retaliation in response to trade disputes—risks termination of these arrangements as well as broader fallout to bilateral relationships. The best argument against unilateral abrogation of the Bosnian arms embargo was that it would have encouraged others to do the same vis-à-vis Iraqi sanctions or in some other context. Coercing others to join sanctions against third parties lest they themselves become the object of unilateral U.S. sanctions—as the Reagan administration did in the early 1980s over European participation in a pipeline that was to bring gas from the Soviet Union, and as Congress did in the mid-1990s to discourage economic activity in Cuba, Iran, and Libya—similarly risks causing major political and economic problems with allies and others. If we pay a price for multilateralism, we also receive dividends; if we see an advantage in unilateralism, we also must be sensitive to its costs.

In certain areas, such as allocation of radio and television spectra or cooperation on global environmental problems, unilateralism is impractical. Similarly, sanctions and supplier clubs meant to stem proliferation by denying key technologies almost always require broad cooperation to be effective. Unilateral action in these realms risks being ineffectual except when the U.S. component is so central that doing without or finding a substitute supplier is not a viable option for the target state. Increasingly, though, such U.S. dominance in the economic realm is rare, as others can provide comparable technologies, large markets, and substantial amounts of capital.

In most instances unilateralism is neither wise nor sustainable. Most military interventions, for example, require either the indirect or direct support and participation of others. Access to bases, the right to overfly, intelligence support—all are usually necessary if an action is at all complicated or distant. Those operations that promise to be large in scale and/or long-term need the active participation of others—their forces and equipment—for several reasons: to share the military burden, distribute economic costs, and assuage domestic political demands that the United States not assume a disproportionate share of the costs of acting in the world when the interests of others are engaged alongside our own. (It was for these reasons that the decision was made to seek contributions to defray the cost of the Gulf War.) Indeed, unilateralism tends to be more popular in principle than in reality. Being costly in blood and treasure, it is unlikely to appeal to Congress and the American people.

The support of others for an intervention or policy can also help politically in other ways. The endorsement of a course of action by the United Nations or a relevant regional body can add an aura of legitimacy and, in the eyes of some, legality to an undertaking. This can have several advantages: fostering domestic political support, bringing about the military and economic participation of others, reducing resistance by the target government or its backers. This was the case in the Gulf conflict, when reliance on the United Nations helped generate international and domestic support for the decision to use force to liberate Kuwait. A pattern of seeking such international endorsement can also help erect a barrier against intervention by those who would abuse their power. Russia, for one, might think twice before dispatching forces to its "near abroad" if it knew that failure to secure a Security Council resolution made it more likely that criticism and even sanctions would follow.

Thus, despite its undeniable domestic political appeal, unilateralism is in most instances not a realistic foreign policy orientation for this country. Unilateralism is not a form of leadership that presumes the willing participation of others but an alternative to it. Aside from those isolationists or minimalists who reject any foreign policy orientation, either because they discount the importance of overseas interests or see a necessity to focus domestically (or both), the real choice facing this country in the foreseeable future is not between unilateralism and multilateralism but between various forms of the latter.

INSTITUTIONALISM

This third approach actually covers a range of options that have in common a commitment to build international bodies and arrangements with authority to meaningfully affect international relations in all spheres. Where such proposals or charters differ is in degree, that is, in the powers and capabilities that are either sought or accorded such institutions. Organizations can range from the relatively modest, promoting coordination where consensus exists, to the ambitious, acting even when some of its members do not concur.

Building such institutions or empowering existing ones, in the process making them a more central vehicle for this country's foreign policy, thus becomes a major foreign policy choice. It was articulated early in the first Clinton administration by Madeleine Albright, then the U.S. permanent representative to the United Nations. "Assertive multilateralism" was the favored phrase.[8]

In principle, an institutional approach to multilateralism has several components. It reflects confidence in the ability of such institutions to function effectively—and the necessity of their doing so. It also tends to reflect a desire that the United States remain involved in the world but at a substantially reduced cost. And it reflects a sense that the potential for international cooperation is great across a broad range of issues, and that the United States can and should work with international organizations in as many instances as possible. Such institutionalism is the contemporary expression of the historic sentiment behind the League of Nations and the United Nations.

An ambitious or expansive form of institutionalized multilateralism would go beyond the initial and apparently abandoned impulse of the Clinton administration. In the security realm, it would involve creating a standing force responsible to the U.N. Security Council and, in some circumstances, to the secretary general. Such a force could in theory be dispatched quickly to help prevent conflicts or (under Chapter VII of the U.N. Charter) to enforce Security Council resolutions. An expanded multilateralism of this sort could also seek to establish machinery (a strengthened International Court of Justice, for example) for resolving political disputes between states that in some instances would constitute binding arbitration, not just mediation. Economically, this form of multilateralism would require not simply rules regulating trade but mandatory dispute-settlement mechanisms and strict monetary coordination. In the environmental area, one could imagine a body that would set standards for individual countries and companies to follow.

The advantage of such institutionalism is that it would put into place machinery for coping with a wide range of global problems, from classic aggression to failed states. The United Nations, for example, has carried out a host of successful peacekeeping operations around the world. The goal would be for it to assume a more demanding role. In addition, the existence of such machinery would ease the burden on the United States, while erecting a constraint against unwanted unilateralism by others.

There are obvious difficulties with multilateralism of this kind. National sovereignty may be much battered but it is still alive and kicking. Few governments (notably our own) would be prepared to cede to some agency (run by international civil servants) the independence they enjoy in the political, economic, or military domains. Moreover, even if there were some desire to do so, it would be an enormous task to create the needed capacities—they do not now exist in the security realm—to do the job. Given the proliferation of weaponry, conflicts, and other forms of instability, the capacities of the United Nations are unlikely ever to be up to handling most of the challenges sure to arise in the post–Cold War world. Bosnia was but one powerful reminder of this reality. Just as important, effective institutionalism requires widespread agreement among the major powers over what needs to be done. Such agreement—tantamount to a concert—does not exist now and is unlikely to for the foreseeable future. To delegate such power to international institutions in the absence of such a concert is to invite inaction and its consequences.

Less unrealistic and considerably more desirable is a scaled-down version of multilateralism, one that would still try to develop stronger and more independent international institutions but with limited powers and for narrow purposes. Robert Keohane makes the case for this more modest form of multilateralism: "Institutions that facilitate cooperation do not mandate what governments can do; rather, they help governments pursue their own interests through cooperation."[9] Such institutionalism tends to be the most appealing and practical in relatively "technical" endeavors; peacekeeping and purely humanitarian operations come to mind. In both instances, the context is consensual and the demands on military capability modest. This is the sort of operation the United Nations has carried out effectively for decades and should continue doing. Such a division of labor would free up U.S. forces for more demanding peacemaking and combat operations and for situations where politics are sure to preclude the emergence of an international consensus. Similarly, the United States and the rest of the world would benefit from putting into place arrangements that would increase the ability of the international community (including both governments and NGOs) to respond to humanitarian tragedies.

The same logic argues for international arrangements in such fields as transportation, communications, and patent and copyright protection where we desire and benefit from a degree of regulation. It also applies to trade, where expanding the scope and coverage of the dispute-settlement mechanisms of the WTO would lubricate trade relations and help insulate bilateral relationships from inevitable disagreements. A stronger and more effective WTO would also be preferable to basing trade on regional arrangements, which could all too easily restrict the movement of goods and services between regions.[10] The International Monetary

Fund and the World Bank are examples of effective institutions that act quasi-independently at the same time that they reflect in voting decisions sovereign concerns and national financial contributions made by members. Environmental arrangements by which states voluntarily agree to abide by certain standards or limits (such as on emissions that cause global warming) have the potential to be beneficial.[11] The International Energy Agency provides a mechanism for sharing energy supplies during times of shortage.

Yet other areas of functioning institutionalism are so-called supplier groups—coalitions of states that agree not to provide designated technologies or capabilities to selected states in order to slow their efforts to develop certain military capacities. Right now there are supplier groups in the realm of nuclear, biological and chemical, dual-use, and ballistic missile technologies. They operate much as cartels, their effectiveness depending on the extent of their reach, i.e., what it is they agree not to export and whether non-members are able and willing to provide what they are not. The result is that institutionalism is a useful component of a foreign policy of regulation that should be expanded where political consensus exists and capabilities can be created or pooled.

POSSES

A third approach to multilateralism is more informal. It differs from alliances and institutionalism in its eschewal of formal organizations and not requiring broad or complete consent. At its core is the idea of selected nation states coalescing for narrow tasks or purposes—and in some cases disbanding once the specific aim has been accomplished. Membership is open to those able and willing to participate. As a result, this approach is sometimes referred to as "coalitions of the willing." Less formally, it is described as foreign policy by posse.

Examples of this approach are multiplying. The most famous case and in some ways the model for the idea are operations Desert Shield and Desert Storm. Here, in response to a specific crisis—the Iraqi invasion and occupation of Kuwait—the United States fashioned a multilateral coalition that over seven months proved victorious on the battlefield. Like many inventions, it was born of necessity: there was no standing Gulf security organization to fall back upon, the crisis fell outside NATO's area of competence, the United Nations lacked the capability, and the demands were too much for the United States alone to undertake.

In the Gulf coalition, tasks and roles differed according to the desire and ability of governments to make a contribution. Some countries simply voted in one or another forum for action against Iraq. Others limited their active participation to providing funds. In the military realm there was a wide disparity. The United States contributed more than a half-million troops and equipment of all sorts. Great Britain and France also committed sizable and varied forces. Other states, for political or military reasons or both, contributed much smaller forces and sometimes only for particular missions—say, sanctions enforcement or defense of rear areas. NATO headquarters contributed meaningfully. The U.N. Security Council's authorization enhanced the undertaking's political and legal appeal, making it easier for governments to join the common effort.

The coalition that won the war disbanded as soon as it ended. But a more narrow coalition (that includes various U.N. bodies) continues to work together in the war's aftermath to promote Iraqi compliance with various resolutions, enforce sanctions, and protect Iraqi citizens from their own government. The United States, Turkey, and Great Britain operate over Iraq's north to monitor Iraq's treatment of the Kurds,[12] while the United States, together with Great Britain, France, and several Gulf states, maintain a similar no fly zone over the predominantly Shia areas of Iraq's south. Both efforts are undertaken "pursuant to" authority judged to be implicit in Security Council resolutions in what amounts to a collective decision to act.

Ad hoc coalitions are also popping up in the economic sphere. The Mexican bailout is an interesting case in this regard. Viewing the potential failure of the Mexican economy as a major threat to world economic health and judging that no existing institution or set of arrangements could provide the Mexican government the required backing, the Clinton administration lashed together in early

1995 an ad hoc coalition that included (in addition to itself) the International Monetary Fund, the Bank for International Settlements, Canada, a consortium of Latin American governments, and private banks. Although the private banks subsequently dropped out, the multibillion dollar bailout appears to have allowed Mexico to weather the immediate crisis.

Diplomacy increasingly turns to informal coalitions. The management of the Middle East peace process since the October 1991 Madrid Conference, coordinated by the United States (with Russia as nominal cosponsor), involves not only the immediate protagonists but also Egypt, the Gulf states, the European Union, and others. Similarly, diplomacy toward Bosnia is informally coordinated by a contact group consisting of the United States, Russia, France, Great Britain, and Germany. An earlier contact group that included the United States, Great Britain, France, Canada, and the then Federal Republic of Germany helped negotiate a political settlement in southern Africa in the 1980s.[13]

Yet another informal coalition was brought about by the October 1994 "Agreed Framework" between the United States and North Korea, which established the Korean Peninsula Energy Development Corporation (KEDO). The United States is in charge, with the Republic of Korea and Japan in principal supporting roles and many other governments in much lesser capacities. The purpose is to provide light-water reactors and alternative energy (in this case, heavy fuel oil) to the North Koreans on terms they can afford in exchange for their forgoing a nuclear weapons option.

What these and similar efforts have in common is that they tend to be U.S.-led groups that come together for a limited set of tasks. (I say "tend" because not all such efforts have been led by the United States—Cambodia comes to mind—and there is no reason all need to be in the future.) They are voluntary as regards membership in general and involvement in particular actions. Their charter is their own. They are often for a limited span of time. They possess little or nothing in the way of headquarters or permanent staff, although they often draw on existing alliances and international institutions. They are better understood as an activity than an organization.

It is not difficult to imagine other applications. Bosnia is one. Rather than trying to force policy through a divided NATO or a United Nations with a different set of priorities, the United States would have been wiser to build a small coalition of like-minded states that would have been in a position to threaten credibly and carry out military actions ranging from making the designated safe areas safe to the so-called lift-and-strike option combining arms supplies to the Bosnians and attacks on Bosnian Serb positions. Some form of ad hoc coalition may well prove useful in the future to help preserve peace (if not justice) in the wake of the departure of NATO forces.

Taiwan is another possibility. If China threatened or used military force against Taiwan, the United States could not hope to get the U.N. Security Council to act, given China's veto. Instead, the United States would have to take the lead in fashioning a coalition of countries to convince China not to use force—and to come to Taiwan's assistance if it did. Ideally, such a coalition would consist of Taiwan, several other states in the region, India, and some European states with power-projection capabilities.

Similarly, the United States would likely have to forge a small coalition including Japan and South Korea as well as others to deal with North Korea's nuclear program, if the current negotiated approach comes up short. This could prove the best way to tackle sanctions if the certain delay and possible Russian or Chinese veto of a Security Council vote were to be avoided. It would be unavoidable if military action were taken. Much the same would apply if the United States undertook military action against emerging unconventional weapons capabilities in Iran or Iraq. Given the controversial nature of preventive strikes, both as regards the act itself and the risk of retaliation against states near the target, it will almost always be necessary for the United States to create posses for such tasks. The same can be said of special sanctions regimes where something more formal or universal is simply not a realistic option to pursue, given opposition in the Security Council or among major trading partners of the target state.

Obviously, the informal coalition approach is not without significant drawbacks. By definition, such groups do not exist before the problem or crisis emerges. They therefore offer no deterrent—although, if formed quickly enough, they can still provide a preventive function. Informal coalitions take time to forge. (Not every protagonist will be like Saddam Hussein and provide months for a coalition to form and get up to speed.) The lack of common equipment, military doctrine, and common experience is likely to limit effectiveness. So, too, will the lack of resources. It is difficult if not impossible to imagine additional bailouts on the scale of Mexico being arranged in an ad hoc fashion. Posses will often lack clear political or legal authority and a means of financing. The United States will more often than not have to provide the bulk of the impetus and resources. As is the case with any variant of multilateralism, informal coalitions constrain. The Gulf War demonstrates that both strategic aims and tactical choices need to be negotiated among coalition members.

There is also the concern that others will follow suit and that a world of multiple sheriffs and numerous posses will be inherently unstable and conflict-prone. One can in principle imagine a number of would-be regional sheriffs: India in south Asia, Germany in Europe, Japan or China in east Asia, Brazil in South America, South Africa and Nigeria in Africa, Iran and Iraq in the Persian Gulf, Israel in the Middle East, and so on. Almost none of these countries would be accepted by its neighbors. Indian hegemony in south Asia is unacceptable to Pakistan; Israeli hegemony is unacceptable to Arab states, as is that of either Iran or Iraq. The Asia-Pacific is filled with multiple candidates who would resist one another.

Some analysts suggest that the corollary to such arguments is that the United States should be precluded from acting in this vein in the absence of a Security Council authorization.[14] Otherwise, it is argued, American-led posses will be nothing more than self-appointed vigilantes. But such a requirement would effectively hand the other four members of the council a veto over U.S. options. What counts the most are the inherent purposes of any action and the steps undertaken toward those ends. The approval of the United Nations is not required to intervene or legitimate any foreign policy—any more than the lack of approval necessarily makes it illegitimate.

Some might object to this approach because it would ask too much of the United States. But a sheriff is not a lone actor or one with infinite resources. He must be willing to work with others and be discriminating in where and how he engages.

The United States should be willing to promote regulation on the basis that the ends and means of what it does will be understood and supported by most. Those who disagree with what we do may withhold support from the enterprise or resist, although there would likely be consequences to either course. Those who want to act similarly—that is, be sheriffs or members of posses of others—are free to do so, understanding that the United States and others retain the option to withhold support or resist their initiatives.

The United States has the potential capacity to create posses where and when it chooses to.[15] For this capacity to be real, however, the United States needs to retain the ability to participate in a significant way. Just as important, the United States needs to continue to cultivate potential partners. Formal alliances may not be as central as they once were, but alignments and allies are. There is thus no substitute for regular and intimate consultations with other governments.

The core justification for posses or coalitions of the willing—and one that outweighs the drawbacks—is that such an approach to international engagement reflects the basic personality and characteristics of a deregulated world.[16] This is a time when multiple great powers are involved in relationships that resist clear definition and range from the cooperative to the competitive at the same time, a growing number of small and medium-size sovereign entities, proliferating regional and international bodies, as well as nongovernmental organizations, an increasing diffusion of power in all its forms, and new sorts of problems (or old problems on a new scale) for which institutions do not yet exist or which they are not prepared to handle. What is needed is an inherently flexible approach to foreign policy that can respond to unforeseen situations in unprecedented ways. Coalitions bring with them some of the advantages that derive from collective effort (resources, specialization, etc.) without the need for consensus or prearranged authority. They also enjoy some measure of international legitimacy.

None of this is meant to exaggerate the strengths of posses. Its weaknesses have already been noted. Posses are better understood as necessary rather than ideal. The goal of foreign policy ought to be to promote norms and build institutions and other arrangements wherever need, consensus, and capability exist. Fortunately, the posse approach can become more structured and institutionalized if warranted and possible. The supplier groups already mentioned reflect this potential, as does the G-7, which over the years has evolved into a quasi institution for managing political and military as well as economic challenges. The WTO represents evolution from previous trade arrangements and promises to evolve more over time. More formal arrangements—including stricter requirements on the data governments must provide the IMF and increasing the IMF's capacity to assist governments at times of balance-of-payments crisis—should be put in place to prevent and, if need be, contend with future "Mexicos."[17] Some regulation of global financial markets, including transfer taxes that should discourage speculation and rapid, frequent shifts of funds in and out of markets, might be in order.[18] An improved IAEA to cope with the challenge of nuclear proliferation would obviously be desirable. It may prove possible to adapt or expand the role of other regional or international institutions.

Again, though, there will be limits in what we can predict and what we can prepare for, especially in the military realm. The absence of consensus on major issues—the absence of a concert of the great powers—limits what can be expected from institutionalism and creates the need for posses. The need for posses, one hopes, will decline—the need for the sheriff to saddle up, one hopes, will diminish as the world becomes more regulated—but history and realism combine to strongly suggest that the need will not disappear, especially in the realm of security.

This is, in any event, a question for the long term. For the immediate future, the real question hanging over the promise of posses is not so much their utility as the willingness and ability of the United States to lead and participate. A posse without a strong sheriff is more likely to sit on its hands or get into trouble than act and accomplish something of value. Strength, however, is a direct result of resources. The United States can be an effective leader only if it has the tools and the will to wield them. For this reason, the subject of the next chapter is what a foreign policy of regulation will require in the way of tools if it is to have a chance of succeeding.

NOTES

1. Josef Joffe wrote a marvelous article in which he compares the choices facing NATO to those confronting a business. Joffe argues that alliances can go out of business, downsize, develop new products for their classical market, or find new markets for their classical product. In NATO's case, he advocates downsizing, much the same as is argued here. See his "Is There Life After Victory? What NATO Can and Cannot Do," *National Interest*, no. 41 (Fall 1995), 19–25.
2. Ronald D. Asmus, Rich L. Kugler, and F. Stephen Larrabee, "Building a New NATO," *Foreign Affairs* 72, no. 4 (September–October 1993), 31.
3. One set of authors has proposed that NATO take on added burdens outside Europe (in both the Persian Gulf and in fighting proliferation) in exchange for a U.S. agreement to provide ground forces to future intra-European conflicts such as we are witnessing in Bosnia. See Ronald D. Asmus, Robert D. Blackwill, and F. Stephen Larrabee, "Can NATO Survive?" *Washington Quarterly* 19, no. 2 (Spring 1996), 79–101.
4. There is a vast literature on the subject of NATO enlargement. Two short pieces that make the case for enlargement are Henry Kissinger, "NATO: Make It Stronger, Make It Larger," *Washington Post*, January 14, 1997, A15, and Stephen Rosenfeld, "To Protect What Is Ours," *Washington Post*, December 27, 1996, A24. Expressions of administration support include Madeleine Albright, "Enlarging NATO: Why Bigger is Better," *Economist*, February 15, 1997, 21–23; Strobe Talbott, "Russia Has Nothing to Fear," *New York Times*, February 18, 1997, A25; and Text of a Letter from the President to the Chairmen of the Senate Committees on Foreign Relations and Armed Services and the House Committees on International Relations and National Security, February 24, 1997. The most developed case against expansion has been put forward by Michael Mandelbaum. See his *The Dawn of Peace in Europe* (New York: Twentieth Century Fund, 1996). A short summary of his thinking on the subject, "Don't Expand NATO," is in *Newsweek* (December 23, 1996), 33.
5. Josef Joffe, "Is There Life After Victory? What NATO Can and Cannot Do," *National Interest*, no. 41 (Fall 1995), 22.
6. For a proposal that the NATO alliance be disbanded and replaced with a new, all-European institution that would also replace the EU and include Russia, see Charles A. Kupchan, "A More Perfect Atlantic Union," *Washington Post*, April 18, 1996, A25. For a discussion of institutional reform in Europe, including but not limited to an expanded NATO, see Christoph

Bertram, *Europe in the Balance: Securing the Peace Won in the Cold War* (Washington, D.C.: Carnegie Endowment for International Peace, 1995).

7. The text of the joint U.S.-Japanese Declaration on Security (signed in Tokyo on April 17, 1996) is in *U.S. Department of State Dispatch* 7, no. 17 (April 22, 1996), 200–201.

8. For background, see Richard N. Gardner, "The Comeback of Liberal Internationalism," *Washington Quarterly* 13, no. 3 (Summer 1990), 23–39.

9. Robert O. Keohane, *After Hegemony: Cooperation and Discord in the World Political Economy* (Princeton, N.J.: Princeton University Press, 1984), 246.

10. See the *Economist* (December 7, 1996), 15–16, 21–23.

11. The United States announced its willingness to do just this in July 1996. See John H. Cushman Jr., "In a Shift, U.S. will Seek a Binding Agreement by Nations to Combat Global Warming," *New York Times*, July 17, 1996, A6.

12. For several years, this operation ("Provide Comfort") also had a substantial ground presence that facilitated the work of numerous humanitarian organizations. This changed in the wake of the events of autumn 1996, when Saddam's forces entered the north at the request of one Kurdish faction. Once the crisis passed, France dropped out of the effort in the north, which in any event was scaled back and renamed "Northern Watch."

13. For background, see Chester A. Crocker, *High Noon in Southern Africa: Making Peace in a Rough Neighborhood* (New York: Norton, 1992).

14. This requirement for U.N. backing is the principal flaw in many ideas being promoted for common or cooperative security or a new concert. See, for example, Charles William Maynes, "A Workable Clinton Doctrine," *Foreign Policy*, no. 93 (Winter 1993–94), 3–20, and Morton Halperin, "Guaranteeing Democracy," *Foreign Policy*, no. 91 (Summer 1993), 120.

15. Other writers have used different but not dissimilar images to describe a post–Cold War role for the United States. See, for example, Paul Nitze, "America: The Honest Broker," *Foreign Affairs* 69, no. 4 (Fall 1990), 1–14; Josef Joffe, "'Bismarck' or 'Britain'? Toward an American Grand Strategy After Bipolarity," *International Security* 19, no. 4 (Spring 1995), 94–117; and Alberto R. Coll, "America as the Grand Facilitator," *Foreign Policy*, no. 87 (Summer 1992), 47–65. For a somewhat more ambitious approach, that the United States become "the global hegemon of the regional hegemons, the boss of all the bosses," see James Kurth, "America's Grand Strategy: A Pattern of History," *National Interest*, no. 43 (Spring 1996), 3–19.

16. Samuel Huntington, whose world of civilizational divisions is quite different from my own age of deregulation, nevertheless argues that "In the emerging world, states and groups from two different civilizations may form limited, ad hoc, tactical connections and coalitions to advance their interests against entities from a third civilization or for other shared purposes." Samuel P. Huntington, *The Clash of Civilizations and the Remaking of World Order* (New York: Simon & Schuster, 1996), 207.

17. On this, see C. Fred Bergsten and C. Randall Henning, *Global Economic Leadership and the Group of Seven* (Washington, D.C.: Institute for International Economics, 1996), 134–38; Paul R. Masson and Michael Mussa, *The Role of the IMF: Financing and Its Interactions with Adjustment and*

Surveillance (Washington, D.C.: International Monetary Fund, 1995); and Jacob M. Schlesinger, "IMF Drafts Plan to Avert Another Mexico," *Wall Street Journal*, December 31, 1996, A4.

18. Chile is experimenting with just this sort of thing. For a general discussion of this problem and potential ways of dealing with it, see Will Hutton, "Relaunching Western Economies," *Foreign Affairs* 75, no. 6 (November-December 1996), 8–12.

Chapter 5

The Tools of Foreign Policy

A new paradigm of international deregulation, a new doctrine of regulation, a new emphasis on temporary coalitions led by the United States when and where multilateral institutions cannot be put in place or made to work—these constitute basic elements of a new American foreign policy for the world after the Cold War. They are all necessary, but even together they are insufficient. What is missing are the tools that make possible specific policies.

THE FOUR BASIC TOOLS

Four tools are central to the successful functioning of foreign policy: defense, intelligence, foreign assistance, and diplomacy. They are not so much choices as components, to be used in conjunction with one another rather than in isolation. The principal problem facing American foreign policy and those entrusted with its implementation in the age of deregulation is how to blend these instruments at a time when they are short on resources, direction, or both.

Resources—or, rather, the relative lack of them—are an immediate and growing problem. As noted above, total annual spending on national security (embracing these four tools) comes to just

103

under $300 billion. It represents about one-fifth of the federal budget, or just under 4 percent of our GNP. This is a great deal but less imposing when the figure is broken down and examined in context. Some shortfalls are more severe and significant than others. Current and projected levels of U.S. defense spending are on the order of $265 billion a year, a figure that subsumes an estimated $28 billion that is devoted annually to intelligence. Both numbers represent a real (inflation-adjusted) decline of some 30 to 40 percent in U.S. spending in these areas over the past decade. Still, it is possible to make the case that the overall level of spending in these areas is adequate (or close to being so) given the reduced threat from abroad. Any significant shortages stem more from specific choices as to how this money is spent than from how much is made available overall.

Spending on foreign assistance and diplomacy is of a different order of magnitude. Despite polls indicating that many Americans believe the U.S. government devotes upwards of 15 percent of its expenditures to foreign assistance programs, the reality is that such programs amount to only 1 percent of federal spending. Over the previous decade, U.S. spending in this area fell by more than a third in real terms. An even starker statistic is that annual spending on foreign assistance—some $14 billion—is just over one-tenth of 1 percent of GNP. This percentage places the United States, for decades the leader in international aid giving, last among the 21 most developed countries.[1] Expenditure on diplomacy is even less, amounting to between $4 billion and $5 billion a year. The State Department employs fewer than 25,000 people in the United States and around the world, making it one of the smaller cabinet agencies. Budget cuts have required the closing of dozens of diplomatic, consular, and cultural posts and aid missions.[2]

Are these resource levels appropriate? In particular, why do we need to spend what seems to be so much on defense? Many critics argue that we should not, pointing out the demise of the Soviet Union and the threat it posed, the low likelihood of hostilities between the United States and any other great power, the weak Russian military showing in Chechnya, and the fact that U.S.

spending on defense far exceeds the combined amount spent by our friends or by any conceivable collection of adversaries.

All this is true, but it is only part of the truth. The United States spends most of what it does on defense because of its broad interests and the wide array of actual and potential threats.

The United States needs to maintain a robust and diverse inventory of nuclear weapons to provide basic deterrence against nuclear attack by Russia or anyone else. This threat is much reduced, allowing a considerably smaller nuclear capability than was required during the height of the Cold War. But the Russians still maintain tens of thousands of nuclear weapons, and a U.S. arsenal is necessary to guard against developments there and in other critical regions where allies would be concerned and adversaries emboldened if U.S. nuclear capabilities atrophied substantially. Although dramatic reductions in the number of U.S. nuclear weapons might be desirable in a context of parallel Russian and Chinese cuts, eliminating U.S. nuclear weapons might actually increase the frequency of nonnuclear wars and increase the incentive of other countries to become nuclear "powers" themselves by fielding just a few devices. For these reasons, calls for the abolition of nuclear weapons are seriously misguided.[3]

The United States also needs to continue to be able to respond to specific threats to its interests. The most demanding and imaginable scenarios involve a war on the Korean peninsula (triggered by a North Korean invasion of the Republic of Korea or possibly the collapse of the impoverished North and massive refugee flows) or an attack by Iran or Iraq upon Kuwait, Saudi Arabia, or several other Gulf states. Although in both theaters the United States would find itself alongside allies, the U.S. component of the response would need to be extensive. Anything less could produce massive instability in two of the world's most critical regions. In Asia and the Pacific, Japan, China, and other powers would all accelerate their rearming and rush to fill the vacuum left by a U.S. retreat. Such a competition could easily threaten the prosperity of a region at the heart of the world economy. In the Gulf, we could find ourselves cut off from oil or at least paying a premium for it. Moderate Arab regimes could become an endangered species;

there is no way they could or would stand up to Iran or Iraq, absent clear U.S. backing. At the same time, Israel would have to brace for a new era of conflict against Iran or Iraq or both.

In addition to these military scenarios—often termed medium regional contingencies or "half-wars" (as opposed to a full war against a rival great power)—there is the relatively remote possibility of an even larger war involving a resurgent Russia moving against Eastern Europe; this would require the United States (and a reenergized NATO) to contain the challenge, much as we did during the Cold War. A skirmish with China could also occur if the mainland were to use force against Taiwan.

U.S. military requirements also include preparing for several smaller contingencies, including hostage rescues, punitive attacks against state supporters of terrorism, preventive attacks against the unconventional weapons sites of rogue states, and interdiction to enforce sanctions or block entry into the United States of drugs and illegal immigrants. There is as well the need to contribute to both peacekeeping (in the Middle East and possibly elsewhere) and selected peacemaking and humanitarian operations, such as in Bosnia, Haiti, Panama, Grenada, Somalia, and Liberia.

Clearly, all these situations occurring at once would overtax any conceivable level of U.S. capabilities—and require a higher level of forces than existed at any time during the Cold War. Indeed, the most critical question affecting force sizing is the assumption about simultaneity. Some argue that planning for one half-war and several smaller demands simultaneously is adequate, noting that no second war erupted when the United States was involved in combat in Korea, Vietnam, or Kuwait. Others argue that planning must assume two half-wars occurring at the same time, either because of coincidence or calculation by one rogue state to exploit American preoccupation with another.[4]

Like many debates, this one is partly theological. The United States has not had the ability to fight two half-wars at full tilt in two theaters simultaneously for some time if ever. A number of critical U.S. capabilities were stretched to the limit by the single half-war in the Gulf. Nevertheless, given U.S. interests in both the Persian Gulf and the Korean peninsula, as well as the existing and potential threats to them, planning for the capability to wage two half-wars with some overlap is warranted to provide a credible deterrent. Moreover, such a capacity allows for a focus on one theater and a holding action in the other, akin to the decision taken during World War II to prosecute the war intensively in Europe before doing so in the Pacific. This force sizing also provides a foundation to build on should a Russian threat to central and Eastern Europe revive or a major Chinese threat materialize in the Asia-Pacific area. This approach allows, too, for the direct and indirect contributions of friends and allies but does not exaggerate what they are able or likely to do. Anything more ambitious on our part would require a quantum leap in defense spending, which would not be supportable politically, and on equipment and ammunition in particular, which would not be supportable strategically. This latter consideration (stemming from the absence of a near-term major threat) argues for devoting a substantial part of available defense dollars on research and development designed to exploit new technologies and to hedge against potential large-scale threats that might emerge.

At the same time, we will need an increasing number of troops and equipment to use in situations other than all-out combat, for those lesser but still highly demanding and dangerous contingencies that increasingly characterize a deregulated world. We do not have the luxury of building two militaries, one for battlefields and one for everything else. But we can emphasize mobility, rapid deployment, and lighter equipment and introduce training for specific missions. We can also invest in "stand-off" systems that let us project power into a situation without establishing a large and potentially vulnerable presence.

The question arises, though, as to why the United States should not simply spend less and wait for its friends and allies to do more. After all, both Japan and Europe could spend considerably more on promoting security and stability. The short answer, however, is that they probably wouldn't—they lack a domestic basis to do more—and we might not welcome it if they did. A relatively modest German and Japanese military effort is not without its reassuring features. And when we do object, we need to keep in mind that we would suffer as well if conflict and misery increased as a result of our doing less and others not acting responsibly. Again, we pay a price—at times a disproportionate one—for what we do in the world, but that price is still affordable in the current context, modest by historical standards, and worth it given the influence it buys and the interests it protects.

It is similarly necessary to explain intelligence costs. Systems for collection of intelligence—satellites, special antennas, and the like—are terribly expensive. There is also a requirement for considerable labor power. But this begs a larger question, which is why have these systems at all? It can be argued that the United States faces much less of a threat than it did only a decade ago and can use free sources of information or pay the price of a magazine subscription.

The reality is more complicated. Despite the end of the Cold War and the abundance of public or readily purchased information, the U.S. government's need for intelligence—defined as information that is not publicly available, or analysis based at least in part on such information that is prepared for policymakers or soldiers—remains great. As a result, no less great is the need for an in-house apparatus entrusted with its collection, production, and dissemination.[5]

Why? Whatever the ultimate personality of the age of deregulation, it will not be an age of global peace and security. The past few years have witnessed classic aggression on a large scale as well as numerous instances of violence resulting from the breakdown of empires and states. Intelligence is essential if military personnel are to cope with such challenges, and it will continue to prove critical in helping government officials fashion and implement policy in any realm that affects national security.

Nor is the need for intelligence eliminated by new sources of information. There are still important but hard to learn facts about targets, including the intentions and capabilities of terrorists and criminal groups, unconventional weapons proliferation efforts carried out secretly by unfriendly governments, and the disposition of hostile military forces. Such information is rarely available on the "information superhighway" or through commercially available satellite imagery; it is certainly not available with enough detail and timeliness to serve policymakers and combatants. Human intelligence—information provided by agents in the field in contact with local sources—is increasingly necessary.

Moreover, the utility of intelligence collection and assessment transcends the continuing need to learn about secrets. It also involves the importance of sorting out mysteries, of analyzing events and trends. Intelligence can often be of greatest use in increasing a policymaker's understanding, rather than in trying to predict individual events. The cadre of analysts maintained by or available to the intelligence community is an important resource for policymakers trying to manage an enormous stream of information. By default as much as by design, the intelligence community is increasingly the locus within the U.S. government where all sorts of information is integrated and related to policy.

Last, intelligence is a tool in two additional ways. Sharing intelligence enables others, be they friendly governments, alliances, or the International Atomic Energy Agency and other U.N. agencies, to be more effective in dealing with challenges that we care about but prefer not to respond to on our own or at all. Many multilateral efforts will succeed only if the United States possesses and is willing to share the necessary means.

The second way that intelligence provides a tool to policymakers is by covert action, operations to influence events in another country in which it is deemed important to hide the hand of the U.S. government. Historically, covert action has included such activities as channeling funds to selected individuals, movements, or political parties, media placements, broadcasting, and paramilitary support. Such operations can bolster friendly governments in dealing with challenges to them and their societies. Covert measures can also have the opposite purpose, to weaken a hostile government. The capability to undertake these and other tasks—be it to frustrate a terrorist action, intercept some technology or equipment that would help a rogue state or group build a nuclear device, or assist some group trying to overthrow a leadership whose actions threaten U.S. interests—constitutes an important national security tool that can provide a valuable alternative or complement to other policies, including diplomacy, sanctions, and military intervention.

Conversely, the question arises as to why we spend so little on assistance and diplomacy. In part, it reflects the end of the Cold War and the inability of successive administrations to justify to Congress and the American public aid and diplomacy expenditures absent a global threat. Foreign aid has never gotten out from under the cloud that it somehow represents giveaways to ungrateful foreigners or incompetent international bureaucrats. Diplomacy has to bear the burden of unfair stereotypes about elite and effete foreign service officers. Moreover, and unlike the military budget or entitlements such as Social Security and Medicare, there is no powerful domestic constituency for either diplomacy or assistance per se, no community to resist the equivalent of a base closing or assembly-line shutdown. (The political constituencies that do exist tend to limit their support for assistance to particular countries, such as Israel or Greece.) Aid and diplomatic accounts thus make a convenient target as pressures mount to balance the federal budget.

Nonetheless, we are talking about a small amount of money by federal government standards. Moreover, in the case of aid, some 80 percent of what is spent actually goes to American companies for the purchase of goods and services. And while it is always possible to point out a degree of waste or fraud in our aid giving, it is also possible to show where such assistance can accomplish real good. Aid, so long as it is properly targeted and conditional, is a valuable foreign policy tool. It can promote exports directly and indirectly through programs (including the Peace Corps) that develop markets. Aid needs to be directed where there are few alternatives and away from regions like Latin America and east Asia, which receive large flows of private capital for investment.

Assistance can also help stabilize new democracies, such as former Soviet republics, where it can also help to secure large stockpiles of nuclear materials. Assistance can make it possible—politically, economically, and militarily—for governments to maintain domestic political support while they make peace. (More than one-third of all U.S. aid goes to Israel and Egypt for this reason.) Assistance funds pay U.N. dues and assessments for peace-keeping forces and other activities, such as those agencies verifying Iraqi compliance with sanctions. Aid also promotes humanitarian welfare, care for refugees, and funds for antiterrorism and anti-drug programs. All these programs are deserving in their own right, promote U.S. foreign policy aims, and ease the burden on other diplomatic tools, the military chief among them.[6]

Diplomacy also has a large potential payoff. One form, arms control, can help reduce the military threat arrayed against this country or at least make it more predictable and visible so that we can better determine our own military requirements and actions. Preventive diplomacy can make conflicts less likely or less pro-longed and violent. It can help make sure that change does not become destabilizing; the ending of the Cold War with hardly a shot being fired, with a unified Germany inside NATO, was any-thing but inevitable.[7] And diplomacy is needed to maintain al-liances and working relationships that are the prerequisites of successful collective efforts.

TOOLS AT WORK

Just as important as the resources for various purposes is how tools are used. Any use of military force or intervention, for ex-ample, must pass several tests if it is to make sense. First, an inter-vention must have a clear and definable purpose to promote or in-terests to protect. Second, an intervention must be doable as well as desirable. Third, the likely benefits of the intervention must be greater than the likely costs. And fourth, this ratio of benefits to costs must be better than that promised to result from other forms of intervention or other policy tools.[8]

Most conceivable classic military interventions—wars in Korea and the Persian Gulf or, on a much smaller scale, hostage rescues and the like—can be designed to meet this standard. His-tory suggests that any use of force for such purposes should be kept narrow in purpose, have ample strength, and be decisive rather than gradual or incremental.

A far more difficult set of choices obtains where U.S. interests tend to be more modest and where the utility of military force tends to be less clear-cut. These situations short of war are characteristic of the age of deregulation. Bosnia, Somalia, Haiti, Rwanda, Liberia, and Burundi all qualify, as would the emergence of other failed states or new civil wars. Such interventions can be designed to be narrowly humanitarian, to provide safety and the basics of life, often through establishment of protected humanitarian zones or safe havens. They can also be more ambitious, be it for nation building (to occupy the country and recast the institutions of the society) or for coercion or peacemaking purposes, which involve a major military effort and tilting the balance in favor of a contending individual or group. Here history strongly suggests that if the United States does intervene militarily, it must have a keen appreciation that domestic tolerance for costs and above all casualties is extremely low when the interests at stake are perceived to be modest. Any intervention must be designed and implemented with this in mind to have a chance of sustaining domestic support.[9]

Using intelligence resources wisely is no less complicated. Throughout most of the Cold War, the intelligence community had the responsibility (one is tempted to say luxury) of focusing the bulk of its resources and efforts on collecting and analyzing information related to the Soviet Union and Eastern Europe. This emphasis was both understandable and necessary, given the nuclear and conventional military strength of the Soviet bloc and its ability to threaten the United States and vital U.S. national interests.

There is no such obvious orientation in the age of deregulation. Thus it is critical that intelligence priorities reflect issues in which U.S. interests are considerable and the threats to them real, and where there is no timely and comprehensive open or commercial alternative. A list of intelligence priorities might include the status of nuclear weapons and materials throughout the former Soviet Union; political and military developments in China, Iraq, Iran, and North Korea; potential terrorism against U.S. targets in the continental United States and overseas; and unconventional weapons proliferation. A second category of important but somewhat lower-priority intelligence targets would include political developments in Russia and relations between Russia and the former Soviet republics; Mexican stability; the stability of Egypt and Saudi Arabia; Indo-Pakistani relations; developments affecting Middle East peace negotiations; and the activities of international criminal organizations. Political and military developments in Bosnia and elsewhere in the Balkans (or any other locale for that matter) would necessarily be a high priority so long as U.S. military units were involved significantly. Environmental protection, population growth, or general political and economic developments around the world would not normally be a priority for U.S. intelligence collection because open sources are usually sufficient.

Foreign assistance should focus where and in a form that it can make a real and positive difference. It is not simply a question of allocating more aid, although higher levels of assistance are in fact required. We need to avoid the temptation to allocate aid just where there happen to be problems; there is more than a little evidence that aid can actually make problems worse by enabling governments to avoid painful but necessary economic reforms.[10] Assistance should be directed to promote market reforms in situations where the private sector is not yet prepared to act. Besides promoting market reforms, assistance can be targeted or made conditional to encourage responsible environmental policy, fund demilitarization, support moderate political behavior, or buttress diplomatic efforts. Assistance can also empower international institutions to carry out tasks such as peacekeeping, thereby reducing demands on U.S. forces. It is essential in these instances that U.S. oversight be adequate to ensure that the missions make sense and are implemented professionally. It is also essential that assistance be consistent with overall foreign policy priorities and goals; for this and other reasons, it makes sense for the Department of State to absorb the currently autonomous Agency for International Development.[11]

Diplomacy is also a scarce resource. The United States cannot do everything everywhere at once. Effort must be focused where interests or threats are the greatest and where U.S. involvement promises to make a difference. Not every situation is ripe for resolution or even U.S. involvement. The United States can, however, be most places at all times at some level, and maintaining a physical presence in all countries and in major cities is well worth doing. Any experienced policymaker will tell you there is no substitute for having someone on the spot in a crisis. Even in normal times, diplomatic reporting contributes to intelligence, while people on the ground can promote American business, serve American citizens, assist the development of democracy and market economies, and help prevent potential crises rather than just react to them.

The optimal use of tools can best be demonstrated by examining some of the broad challenges facing the United States in the age of deregulation. These can be grouped in two categories: difficult actors and difficult situations. Each is discussed in turn below.

DIFFICULT ACTORS

Difficult actors (including but not limited to countries) are those that threaten the United States and its citizens. The means can be weapons (aircraft or missiles) that can reach U.S. territory or terrorism. Difficult actors are also those that threaten or have the potential to threaten the balance of power in key regions, notably the Asia-Pacific, the Persian Gulf, and Europe. Included in this category are rogue states (Iran, Iraq, Libya, North Korea, possibly Syria), nonallied major powers (China and Russia), and various terrorist organizations.

Intelligence is important in several ways in dealing with the challenges posed by such countries and groups, most of all by simply keeping track of what they are doing and alerting policymakers to any change in their capabilities or intentions. Covert action also has the potential to play a helpful role by thwarting specific development or acquisition efforts related to military capabilities or by interrupting preparations for a terrorist attack. More ambitious but even more difficult to effect (and impossible to count on) is covert action designed to overthrow the leadership of a rogue actor.

Diplomacy has a central role in dealing with difficult actors. It can be used to limit their capabilities. This can be done consensually through arms control agreements, such as those between the United States and Russia limiting inventories of offensive missiles and defensive systems. Arms control also casts a wider net by banning biological and chemical weapons and by seeking to discourage the emergence of new nuclear powers, whether directly (through the Non-Proliferation Treaty) or by a comprehensive test ban that would complicate the process of developing (if not acquiring) a nuclear device. Arms control has less to offer here, though, as rogue states by definition tend to reject international norms or accept them in form only to violate them in fact.

Capabilities can also be affected diplomatically by selective denial. Such agreements are consensual only among the like-minded and are designed to frustrate the "have-nots" in acquiring specific technologies or capabilities. Throughout the Cold War, for example, the Western industrial states maintained a Coordinating Committee (COCOM) to control the flow of technology to the Communist world. Currently, there are several supplier groups consisting of countries that agree to exercise self-restraint in not exporting selected materials that would assist nonmembers in the development of chemical, biological, or nuclear weapons or ballistic missiles. At best, such groups can complicate but not prevent the acquisition of critical technologies. Full global compliance is impossible to bring about in an age of global markets and in the face of determined efforts by rogue actors to acquire critical technologies.

Diplomacy can also affect the behavior of problem actors. The potential exists in certain cases to change what these actors do at home and abroad (if not what they are) by providing incentives and imposing penalties and linking them to particular behavior. Such diplomacy is a critical tool of a foreign policy of regulation.

Manipulation of incentives and penalties or linkage is akin to American efforts to discipline Soviet behavior during the era of détente. But linkage (constructive or conditional engagement, to use the more contemporary phrases) is more easily talked about than implemented. It can be extremely difficult to rally domestic and international support for a restrictive policy, and, without a common front, there is little incentive for the target to behave differently, either toward its own people or its neighbors.

There are several reasons why gaining support for policies of constructive or conditional engagement is so hard. To begin with, denying technology and goods to selected states means accepting lost exports. There is thus an economic price that few businesses and governments are willing to pay.

There is also the political argument that such policies are counterproductive. One hears often that it is better to engage economically than not. At least in principle, trade and interaction can make a closed society more open, strengthen the middle class, and reinforce market changes that in time tend to lead to desirable political changes. This refrain is often voiced by Europeans and Japanese in defending their resistance to isolating Iran or Cuba economically.

Last, we ourselves are ambivalent. Linkage does not operate in only one direction. A willingness to introduce sanctions over one aspect of China's behavior invites Chinese retaliation in an area where we have a stake in the status quo. Similarly, we have interests we want to pursue without conditions. Thus, even if we object to Russia's use of force in Chechnya, we would not want to withhold assistance that would improve the safety of Russian nuclear storage installations.

Many of these arguments can be refuted or at least dealt with in particular instances. Any short-term economic price would be worth paying to avoid a major, costly crisis brought about by a strengthened rogue actor. Moreover, international cooperation means that sales will not be lost to a competitor but simply postponed for everyone. The political argument against conditionality does not stand scrutiny. To invest in or trade with a rogue state in the hope it reforms is naive. Reform is likely to come (if then) only if goods and credits are tightly linked to specific behavior. Last, it is true that linkage can work against as well as for us. But the correct lesson is not never to apply it but to do so with care, when it is likely to effect the change in behavior we seek rather than just be a gesture or, worse, involve costs that the target can better sustain than we can.

Successful diplomacy also requires a correct assessment as to whether the desired behavioral change is likely on the part of the target state. If not, a policy of conditional or constructive engagement cannot succeed. In such cases, the United States must choose among policies of accommodation or isolation.[12]

By contrast, constructive engagement tends to be the best course when desired change is possible or when isolation is judged either undesirable or untenable because of a lack of multilateral support. Here, Iran and Cuba come to mind. In both instances, it is possible to argue that the goal of seeing the country become more democratic and market-oriented (and, in the case of Iran, less threatening) would be facilitated by offering specific economic incentives. What is certain is that the current unilateral U.S. approach cannot provide the necessary leverage. As a result, it makes sense to explore a multilateral approach that ties the willingness of most states to trade and invest to the target's meeting specified standards. If the standards were met, the United States would relax its prohibitions and drop all penalties aimed at third parties; if the standards were not met, then others would agree to reduce or eliminate their economic interaction. Exploring constructive engagement has several advantages. Not only might it work, but even if not, it should make it less difficult to cobble together a united, restrictive front.

Accommodation makes sense when the behavior in question, however undesirable, is tolerable, when there is little or nothing to be done about it, or when other priorities are at stake. Such a decision can reflect the absence of multilateral support or simply the inability to exert effective influence. By contrast, isolation is preferable when the target constitutes a threat and when it demonstrates no interest in changing its behavior for the better. In such situations, an attempt to bring about a change in the nature of the target—rollback or overthrow—may be warranted. Here, both Iraq and North Korea come to mind.

Such isolation is best understood in the economic and security realms. Diplomatic isolation, however, rarely is in our interest. Recognition and the establishment of diplomatic relations ought to be a normal and, as much as possible, a technical decision. When we withhold it because we do not approve of a government, we limit our ability to interact and set up an obstacle to establishing relations should we later judge it in our interest to do so.

Similar arguments apply to consultations, negotiations, and summitry. To the extent possible, all should take place on a regular basis. They are not a favor or reward to be bestowed but a potentially useful means to get our points across and hear our opponents'. As a result, such meetings should not be denied or cancelled as a sanction when a difficult state acts badly. At such moments, a meeting could be more useful than ever.

Economic assistance can serve policymakers at the margins and then only with states in financial difficulty and not considered rogues, in which case giving aid would be unimaginable. Russia would qualify; aid to help authorities there deal with the security and safety of nuclear materials is in our interest as well as theirs. Technical aid to China may make sense in the realm of legal reform or environmental efforts.

How do these considerations affect specific policies? With Russia, the United States requires a multifaceted approach. Diplomacy, notably arms control, must continue to attempt to reduce the number of nuclear weapons and delivery systems. But diplomacy must also include regular high-level exchanges on the full range of issues of concern to each side, including the disposition of Russian nuclear weapons and materials and the terms of NATO enlargement. Constructive or conditional engagement can be attempted to affect external and to a lesser extent internal policies. All this should be done against a backdrop of "latent containment," which requires not simply an American military presence in Europe under NATO but careful diplomatic handling of a country experiencing a wrenching transition. The challenges posed by Russia's complicated mix of residual military strength, economic weakness, and political turbulence will not be easy to meet.

A no less complex blend of policies is required in the case of China. Here, too, constructive engagement is called for. It is premature to embark on a policy of explicit containment. The United States could not sustain it alone. Our allies in the region and beyond, while wary of China's potential strength and its tendency (as shown against Taiwan in March 1996) to use intimidation to get its way, are not prepared to sign on. Even if a policy of containment were to prove necessary, it would be expensive and dangerous. Far better would be a more "bourgeois" China prepared to accept the norms of a regulated world in how it acts at home and beyond its borders.

For now, the United States should adopt a wait-and-see posture, one in which containment mostly would be latent while the potential for Sino-American cooperation is explored by the two governments. Deng Xiaoping's successors need to understand that what they do vis-à-vis issues of concern to the United States—including exports of nuclear materials and ballistic missiles, human rights, Korea, Hong Kong, and Taiwan—will affect what we say and do. Trade issues ought to the extent possible be pushed into the WTO; this argues for making China a member of that organization as soon as it can meet the basic requirements. On Taiwan, the message needs to be clear that no use of force by China will be acceptable under any circumstances. In return, China should know that the United States will not deviate from its one-China policy and that any unilateral action by Taiwan to change its status will go unrecognized. Diplomatic exchanges with China on this and other issues of mutual concern should be regular and unconditional. Such consultations are critical. The United States and China no longer have the Cold War structure of triangular diplomacy and a common Soviet threat as an impetus to cooperate. Managing China's emergence as a great power promises to be the most significant and demanding national security challenge of this era; indeed, how well it is handled could well determine how long the age of deregulation lasts and what succeeds it.[13]

The military tool can make several potential contributions to the effort of contending with problem states. Defending the homeland is the most fundamental. The United States now has the luxury of not facing traditional military threats on its borders or from anyone in the hemisphere. But it does face threats all the same, from terrorism and from long-range missiles belonging to Russia and, to a much lesser extent, China and potentially others.

It is curious that we as a country do little to protect the territory and people of the United States—our greatest interest. This is the result of a conscious decision made during the Cold War that reflected a lack of capability to do much about the danger of missiles and a decision because of that to premise stability on mutual vulnerability. This concept was enshrined in the 1972 Anti-Ballistic Missile (ABM) treaty, which significantly limited the ability of the United States and the Soviet Union to build a national defense against ballistic missiles.

The obvious question is whether such a posture still makes sense. Technology is more promising than was the case a quarter-century ago. Moreover, even though the likelihood of a deliberate Russian attack is much diminished, there is the chance of an accidental or unauthorized Russian strike against the United States and emerging threats from others. Already, North Korea has in development a missile that will be able to threaten Hawaii and Alaska. Sometime in the next century, several countries could pose such a threat to the U.S. mainland.[14]

When threats emerge, if the technology is available, we should field a national ballistic missile defense effort. Acting against a limited, long-range (strategic) threat to the United States would almost certainly require the United States and Russia to amend the 1972 Anti-Ballistic Missile treaty or our abrogating the treaty. Unless done jointly, this would exact a substantial toll on relations with Russia and block any agreement on lower offensive limits. We do not need to make this decision now, although before long we may need to do so, depending on the course of Russian politics, the proliferation of weapons of mass destruction, and technological developments. The ABM treaty has been valuable but it is not sacrosanct. It was meant to enhance stability in one context, the bipolar world of the Cold War. It did this, but in the age of deregulation, the threat and the technology are fundamentally changing. So, too, must our posture.[15]

Defense against terrorism is also exceedingly difficult, if for different reasons. The United States is an open society, and there is no way to control access to every inch of its borders or the actions of every individual once inside the country. Moreover, today's cities, with their concentrated populations, high technology, and dependence on centralized systems of transport, power, and water, make rich targets. We are vulnerable—another feature of the age of deregulation.

What should we do? Physical security measures can help, but they can never be a panacea. Intelligence is crucial. The best way to deal with terrorism is to stop it before it happens. Sharing intelligence with other governments and international agencies can be useful. The need for information is likely to require expanded wiretapping that would entail some limited compromise of civil liberties. Covert action is an option in those rare instances when we have specific information. Punitive military strikes against states sponsoring or harboring terror are another option that can affect their calculation of the benefits and costs of supporting such behavior. A U.S. attack in 1986 seems to have influenced Libya to reduce its support for terrorism, at least for a few years.

The military tool is even more central to dealing with the balance of power in critical regions. The purpose of this policy tool is to deter any use of force by a potential adversary or to defeat it if deterrence fails. In Europe, this argues for a continued American military presence on the ground in NATO. NATO should remain a transatlantic institution but with a greater weighting toward the European side commensurate with Europe's growing strength and the greater demands elsewhere on the United States. Despite all the attention devoted to NATO enlargement, the degree to which NATO can and should "Europeanize" may prove to be the more significant issue over time.[16] The most pressing regional problems, though, are to be found outside Europe in the Persian Gulf, where Iran or Iraq could threaten regional stability, and northeast Asia, where a war triggered by either a North Korean attack or collapse is possible.

To be an effective deterrent, the military tool requires some presence in the region backed up by the ability and a perceived willingness to introduce more and more capable forces there in short order. Such a military posture requires ample conventional military forces, mobility, and close cooperation with friendly local states.

The proliferation of unconventional weapons is a complicating factor here. Their use by adversaries requires U.S. personnel to adopt measures from special equipment to changed tactics that detract significantly from performance. In addition, use of unconventional munitions by foes greatly increases the danger of American casualties. The calculus of intervention—the basic assessment of projected costs and benefits—changes if it includes having to cope with chemical or biological agents or nuclear weapons.

For this and other reasons, the United States has historically done a great deal to discourage the proliferation of weapons of mass destruction. On the diplomatic side, U.S. policy has encouraged countries to adhere to the Nuclear Non-Proliferation Treaty and a comprehensive test ban; the formation of supplier cartels to slow the spread of critical technologies; the provision of conventional weapons and security guarantees to friends to diminish their desire or need to possess nuclear or other unconventional weapons; active conflict resolution designed to reduce the causes of war; and, in the case of North Korea, a buyout by which the United States agreed to provide oil and a new generation of electricity-producing reactors in exchange for North Korea's eliminating its nuclear weapons program. These and other efforts may have slowed proliferation in certain instances, but the United States has not and cannot prevent it in every case. The age of deregulation will be an age of proliferation.

As a result, there are as well military tools, including military action on our part, to prevent the acquisition of capabilities by others. Much as the Israelis did against Iraq in the early 1980s, the United States could conceivably destroy part or all of an emerging unconventional weapons capability. There are problems with such a posture, however. One needs detailed intelligence about the target, often hard to acquire given the secrecy that shields these operations. (It turned out, for example, that neither the United States nor the relevant world oversight agency knew much about either the Iraqi or the North Korean nuclear programs.) There must also be the means to reach and destroy the target, which is often difficult when it is mobile or buried deep underground. Any attack carries with it the risk that the other side will retaliate, possibly initiating a larger war fought with any unconventional weapons not destroyed in the preventive attack.

There is also the political problem that preventive attacks are highly controversial, something that could complicate the task of organizing an international response to the rogue state in the aftermath of the preventive strike. Indeed, where retaliation is an option, it would be unthinkable to launch a preventive strike without the concurrence of countries that would be affected, such as Japan and South Korea in any attack on North Korea.

The bottom line is that preventive attacks are more easily contemplated than carried out. Other strategies are thus designed to limit the likelihood that unconventional weapons would actually be used in a conflict. Again, there is the option of a preemptive strike at the outset of a war. The problem, again, is that it is impossible to have high confidence in success. Diplomacy has something to offer here, however. Deterrence can be enhanced through the private and/or public communication of clear warnings to the adversary of the consequences of using unconventional weapons against U.S. or friendly forces. These consequences include punitive attacks by conventional weapons against valued political and economic targets, possible retaliation in kind, and (in some contexts such as the Korean peninsula, where South Korean forces would provide a natural army of occupation), a message that the war will not be terminated without a change in regime in the aggressor country.[17]

Last, steps can be taken to minimize the impact of unconventional weapons. Options range from protective measures (special clothing against chemicals, vaccines against toxins) to adjustments to the size of formations and support facilities so as to reduce the number of high-value targets. Another potential response—theater defense against ballistic missiles—can exploit advanced technology. Moreover, it should be possible to do this without abrogating the ABM treaty, especially if the United States exploits the latitude inherent in the treaty when it comes to nonstrategic defenses. We should not, however, give the Russians a veto over our plans. Our need to deal with already existing threats in regions vital to us is too important to ignore because of Russian concerns.[18] Again, we need to adapt thinking and behavior developed during the bipolar world of the Cold War for the very different world of deregulation.

DIFFICULT SITUATIONS

Difficult or problem situations include developments inside states (which may or may not be problem states) that pose a threat to interests that are not vital or that merit our attention even though no specific U.S. interests are directly endangered. For various reasons—concern over human rights or physical suffering, opposition to genocide, a desire to prevent or limit conflict within or among states—these situations place pressure on the United States to act.

Intelligence can again play a role in contributing to U.S. policy. There is a problem, though, in that none of the difficult situations qualifies as a vital interest, and as a result it is difficult to justify expending vast intelligence resources on them. Moreover, it is almost impossible to do so beforehand. No one, for example, could have predicted with certainty that 20,000 U.S. soldiers would be deployed to either Haiti or Bosnia.

In this context, intelligence is also important in another way. Sharing it is essential to empowering others to act. In many of these problem situations, the direct U.S. role will be modest. Instead, the United States will largely turn to others, including the United Nations, to carry out certain humanitarian or peacekeeping missions. They will be better able to do so if they have the benefit of intelligence that only the United States can provide.

Diplomacy also is essential if U.S. policy is not to be overwhelmed by these situations. "Preventive diplomacy" can defuse potential conflicts (within or between states) before they erupt. Diplomacy can also keep a bad situation from getting worse. "First do no harm" ought to be the credo of more than doctors. But harm can be done by diplomats who do not think through the consequences of their actions. One important example is in our approach to self-determination and the granting of diplomatic recognition to newly independent states. The powerful, ethnically driven nationalism characteristic of the age of deregulation makes this a life-or-death choice. It is essential to provide recognition only after credible provisions are made to protect minorities. Arrangements for autonomy, federal structures, and legal protection are all potential safeguards. Where states are breaking up, recognition also should be made conditional on the putting into place of arrangements that increase the odds the breakup will be peaceful. The former Yugoslavia is a tragic example of what unconditional recognition can contribute to; by contrast, the divorce between Czechs and Slovaks in the former Czechoslovakia is evidence that divorce need not be violent.

Self-determination cannot be limitless. Not only must there be legitimate cause—Amitai Etzioni has suggested supporting self-determination only when the secessionist movement in question seeks to leave an empire that refuses to democratize[19]—but, more important, it cannot just be declared by the "self." Others directly affected, including minorities within the putative state and neighbors, require and deserve a voice. For this reason, the United States has been correct not to support Palestinian self-determination but only a right for Palestinians to participate in the determination of their own future. Israel and arguably Jordan merit consideration and consultation. Anything else—anything less—would be a prescription for war. Without careful regulation, nationalism and the breakup of the current state system could all too easily lead to the breakdown of international order. Bosnia could be the rule rather than an exception.

Diplomacy also needs to be realistic to prosper. Americans have a penchant for ready solutions, but not every conflict can be solved. In those cases, we would do better to focus on more modest arrangements that help keep the peace and perhaps create conditions when the conflict will be ripe for solution. The Middle East is a good example of how gradualism and interim arrangements can succeed; its lessons arguably are apt for India and Pakistan, who are not about to negotiate a solution to Kashmir, as well as for Greece and Turkey, who disagree over a range of bilateral problems as well as the future of Cyprus.

Similarly, not every ethnic group or cluster of people is ready to live with others. Here Bosnia comes to mind. While multinational societies tend to be more democratic and tolerant, it is virtually impossible to imagine Bosnia's Muslims, Serbs, and Croats agreeing to live with and among one another given the recent violence. Yet this is what the Dayton accord sets out to do. Such a goal risks not only being unrealistic; it could shatter the fragile peace if people actually tried to reclaim their homes and villages. Partition is sometimes the least bad option. Order with justice may always be the most desirable, but order without justice is preferable to no order (and no justice) at all.[20]

Diplomacy can also be enhanced when backed up by economic sanctions. There is an increasing tendency to turn to sanctions as an expression of U.S. outrage or concern but also as an alternative to using military force. And there is some evidence of success. Sanctions may have played a useful role in encouraging white South Africans to end apartheid. And in the former Yugoslavia, one can argue that economic sanctions helped persuade the Serbian government in Belgrade that the time had finally arrived for a diplomatic solution.

But sanctions can also backfire. The ban on arming any protagonist weakened the Bosnian government to the benefit of its Croatian and Serbian neighbors. Sanctions against the antidemocratic government of Haiti actually increased misery on the island as well as the number of boat people—without having much effect on the leadership, which was able to insulate itself to a large extent. The result was to increase the likelihood that the United States would use force. Sanctions, such as those imposed unilaterally against Iran and Cuba, can also cause friction between the United States and its principal friends and allies—an added cost that must be weighed against the likely impact on the target state.

Aid is a critical element in the context of problem situations, far more so than in the case of problem actors. Assistance can be a tool of prevention, to bolster societies economically so they are less likely to disintegrate. Aid can provide resources to political leaders so they can justify the risks and costs of peace and political compromise to their publics. And aid can always carry out its most basic mission—to provide the basics of life when the state can no longer do so.

Aid can also be useful in the military sphere. There are those humanitarian nightmares that are the result not of some act of God but of men. Military aid to friendly governments can help them deal with illegitimate challenges to order, whether internal or from a neighbor. Conversely, military aid can be provided to peoples or groups resisting a tyrannical government. In all these situations, military aid can be an alternative to more direct U.S. military involvement. When aid is not forthcoming in such situations, the choices can easily be reduced to two: staying out or intervening directly with military force. (Sanctions tend to work too slowly if at all.) The former Yugoslavia illustrates this all too well, as a decision against arming the favored local party left the United States with few choices but to intervene directly with airpower and 20,000 troops.

Direct military intervention in problem situations is extremely difficult, though. Many of these situations are violent and have many or all the characteristics of civil war: the absence of a clear battlefield, no sharp line between combatants and civilians, multiple parties with uneven discipline, and deep emotion that frustrates a quick end to fighting. Moreover, what is often missing from these situations are the vital interests that would persuade the public and Congress that going in and sorting things out was worth the inevitable human and financial costs.

One military option that attempts to ameliorate humanitarian problems in a manner that limits costs is the establishment of safe havens. Safe havens are nothing more than zones carved out within a country by outside powers in which people are protected from the central government or a rival ethnic group. The idea is not to assert sovereignty but to deny it to those who abuse its powers or fail to live up to its obligations. Safe havens can be created as a magnet for people or they can be established where the endangered people are already located if they happen to be concentrated in one or only a few places. Military forces are well-suited for maintaining safe havens; as Robert Cooper and Mats Berdal have correctly pointed out, "Foreign forces can keep groups apart more easily than they can bring them together."[21]

To be effective, safe havens require significant air and a modest number of ground forces inside and around them. They also require the establishment (and enforcement) of a weapons-exclusion zone around the area—to place all hostile weapons out of range—and a no-fly zone over them. Air forces must be prepared to carry out disproportionately large punitive attacks on those who violate the area. Such attacks should communicate a sense of seriousness and, over time, help deter future challenges. This approach is akin to what the French did for a time in Rwanda, and what the United States did for several years in northern Iraq and finally in Bosnia in 1995, after allowing two of six cities designated as safe to fall.

Safe havens have some obvious drawbacks. They are open-ended, offering no guaranteed exit date for those who maintain them. They must be policed so that they are not used as basecamps to mount military operations by the protected side. Some pilots and ground troops will be lost in defending them. Except in situations where an endangered population already is concentrated in one area, establishing zones can either fail to protect some people or force them to migrate to safety, thereby rewarding aggressors. They require a degree of consensus and cooperation among the protected; the breakdown of comity in mid-1996 between the two most powerful Kurdish factions of northern Iraq markedly reduced the utility of the safe haven. Most of all, safe havens are limited in what they can accomplish directly. They are designed to provide a respite, not a solution, to the problem at an affordable cost. They are needed until the politics of the situation evolve. Safe havens thus keep people safe while buying time for other approaches—sanctions, covert action, providing arms, diplomacy—to work.

Other, more demanding military options promise to accomplish more but also are sure to cost more. One such tool is coercive military force to affect the calculations (and hence behavior) of a belligerent. At least in principle, such a limited demonstration of military force can persuade the actor—which can be a government, a group, or a neighboring state—to curtail aggression. Coercive interventions tend to work best when their goal is modest. A drawback of this approach is that any coercive use of force that fails yields difficult choices: military escalation or some form of acquiescence. An additional problem is that it leaves the initiative entirely in the hands of the target, who is unlikely to be impressed by a winner-take-all situation (with loser forfeiting all) that is also one in which the United States has only a limited stake.

Peacemaking (not to be confused with peacekeeping, which is more political than military and takes place amid the consent of the local parties) is an even more demanding option that would turn the United States into a protagonist in a conflict. It seeks to defeat rival parties or alter their behavior and can involve the use of force, the threat to use it, or both. The United States and NATO engaged in peacemaking in Bosnia when they attacked Bosnian-Serb positions and then when they entered the country to enforce the Dayton accord in the absence of local consent. Opportunities for successful peacemaking are likely to be rare, however. Vietnam, Lebanon, and Somalia all demonstrated that peacemaking is extremely demanding militarily and difficult to sustain politically, both at home (because of the high costs and uncertain prospects for success) and in the target country, where nationalist pressures, the difficulties of working with disorganized internal forces, and the need to act with great restraint in order not to alienate neutrals must be considered.

Occupation and nation building are still another military option in difficult situations. Nation building can be motivated by how a state treats its own people. It can also be motivated by a desire to transform a state's foreign policy so that it does not again resort to force against neighbors. But nation building is an ambitious enterprise designed to make a country secure and stable—a goal that requires replacing the existing political authority (or creating one where none exists) so that local peoples can lead relatively normal lives. Nation building requires defeating and disarming any local opposition and establishing a political authority that enjoys a monopoly or near-monopoly of control over the legitimate use of force.

Successful nation building can involve first going to war, as in the cases of Japan and Germany in World War II. In both cases, nation building required years of occupation. To succeed, nation building sometimes must seek to do nothing less than remake a political culture. This is clearly the case with the U.S. (and subsequently U.N.) occupation of Haiti. It is more demanding in the near and medium term than humanitarian interventions but potentially less so over the very long term. It is highly intrusive, as even the limited nation building efforts in Panama and Grenada both demonstrate. Opportunities for successful nation building will be rare. Few regimes are that dangerous, and even when they are, we will rarely want to pay the price. It was in part for this reason that the Bush administration decided against undertaking such an ambitious approach to Iraq in the aftermath of Desert Storm.

North Korea appears to be a prime exception because of its demonstrated aggression and the availability of South Koreans to undertake an occupation.

In nearly all these situations, the United States needs to consider not just getting in but also getting out. (The only exception to the need to leave might be where it is both possible and necessary to design a strategy for staying that is justified by the scale of the interests and the threats.) But to consider leaving should not be interpreted as setting a date for doing so in advance. Such an arbitrary approach, however satisfying to domestic opponents of overseas commitments, makes no sense if it only encourages adversaries to hold back until we leave. Rather, what is needed is a strategy that allows a transition to a stable situation, be it one maintained by the local parties themselves or by some other outside force.

How does one know which policy tool to use and which if any military intervention to undertake? There is no hard-and-fast rule when it comes to problem situations. The choice must be shaped by the actual or potential scale of the problem. Not every human rights problem is genocide; not every conflict need escalate. Just as important, the decision to intervene militarily must be based on an assessment that it can provide relief at acceptable costs and promise better results at no greater costs than alternative measures. What should almost always be avoided are limited efforts on behalf of large goals. A decision that ignores any of these factors risks serious problems on the ground as well as at home.

BEYOND PROBLEM STATES AND SITUATIONS

Not all foreign policy questions fit neatly into the two categories of problem states and situations. One that does not is drugs. One can design a foreign policy–oriented strategy for drugs that employs a range of tools. Aid can be dispensed and intelligence shared with cooperative governments to increase their incentive and ability to crack down on producers. Sanctions can be threatened or imposed on governments reluctant to adopt such measures. Military force can be used "to go to the source" and destroy production facilities or to interdict shipments.

All these approaches have been used—and a great deal of money is being spent with only modest effect. Statistics demonstrate that we are increasing the amount of drugs destroyed and intercepted but are making little if any dent in the amount of drugs that enter the United States or, more important, are consumed.[22] Foreign policy sees drugs as essentially a problem of supply, but the reality is that they are more a problem of domestic demand. No amount of foreign policy tools will make much of an impact on demand; resources would better be devoted more to domestic programs for reducing demand and providing treatment.[23]

Energy also demonstrates the limits of foreign policy. The United States is not only the world's largest user of oil and gas but is increasingly dependent on foreign sources of energy. Half of all oil consumed in this country is now imported. Nearly 20 percent of these imports, or just under 10 percent of all oil consumed in the United States, comes from the Persian Gulf. The amount of oil imported and dependence on the Gulf are likely to grow, given falling domestic production, rising consumption, and the fact that the world's greatest untapped reserves are located in the Gulf area. Price could also rise if world demand for oil far outpaced supply, which is likely to happen once Chinese and Indian consumption jumps.[24]

We can do a number of things about this problem, again using multiple tools. Military force can deter and if need be resist attempts by hostile forces to dominate oil-producing regions such as the Persian Gulf. Diplomacy can bring about sharing or pooling arrangements among consumers, such as now exist under the International Energy Agency. Sanctions are maintained against Iran and Iraq, in part to limit their capacity to threaten their immediate neighbors. Companies can and do diversify sources of oil and gas. We maintain and can tap into a domestic reserve at times of supply interruption and price hikes.

But none of these steps can alter the fundamentals of dependence, which strains our economy and distorts U.S. foreign policy. We as a nation pay a price for driving our cars above 55 mph, for preferring gas-guzzling sports utility vehicles to more efficient forms of transport, for resisting the development of offshore areas out of environmental considerations, and for our opposition to higher taxes at the gas pump that would discourage consumption. The result is that we add a great burden to our foreign policy.

Illegal immigration is a third special subject. Again, there are foreign policy undertakings that can alleviate the problem. The most basic might be promoting economic and political reform in neighboring states so there is less reason for people to leave. Aid can be important in this. We can increase our interdiction and screening efforts and even erect physical barriers. But again, there is a limit to what foreign policy can reasonably be expected to accomplish. At some point, coping with immigration becomes a domestic political issue. We can, for example, let more people in legally. We can reduce benefits for those who are not U.S. citizens or who are here illegally. We can introduce stiffer penalties for those who employ illegals. What we cannot do is expect foreign policy to solve the problem for us.

TOOLING UP: SOME CONCLUSIONS

What general conclusions emerge from this consideration of the four basic foreign policy tools of intelligence, diplomacy, assistance, and military force? The first is not to rely exclusively on the military to implement a doctrine of regulation. It is expensive by any measure, and there is only so much of it to go around. It is not appropriate for many tasks or certainly not as appropriate as other instruments. Domestic tolerance for casualties and costs is extremely low when interests are seen as less than vital.

This raises a related, larger point. Earlier in the chapter a set of calculations was presented regarding the use of military force and when it was warranted. A similar calculation applies to any foreign policy tool. One must always ask whether the projected benefits justify the estimated costs, and whether this calculation compares favorably with those of other tools, with doing nothing at all, or with doing something in some combination. Foreign policy is not therapy; its purpose is not to make us feel good but to do good.

The careful mix of tools requires changing how decisions are made. At the national level, economic and other less traditional issues need to be better integrated with other foreign policy concerns. This requires a revamping of the National Security Council so that economic and environmental interests receive stronger but less separate consideration. Within the State Department, a reduction of fiefdoms and single-issue advocates would force senior officials to make trade-offs at all stages of policymaking rather than react to crises in part created by a lack of integrated policy. An added benefit of this reform is the resource savings that would accrue.[25]

A fourth point that emerges from a review of the tools is how many of them must be used with other actors, that is, in a multilateral fashion, if they are to have any chance of succeeding. As argued earlier, the real choice facing American foreign policy today is not between unilateralism and multilateralism but among various forms of the latter. In a global economy, there are fewer and fewer situations where the United States alone can implement an effective policy of denial or economic isolation to deal with a problem. But this also reflects the reality of American politics, that for all our distrust of multilateralism, there are limits to what we are prepared to spend and do. Either we will join with others or empower others, or things that matter to us will not be attended to by anyone. Allies and alignments will tend to matter more than formal alliances. Where possible, we ought to build international organizations and institutions; where not, coalitions are the best alternative.

In a related vein, multilateralism rarely just happens. More often than not, it is the result of American leadership. We cannot dictate to others, but we can influence them. Consultations between the United States and others thus become critical. Here it is essential that we are willing not only to listen but also to lead. We must come to such meetings prepared to propose and work for a course of action. When we don't—as was the case with Bosnia in the spring of 1993, when the United States simply presented ideas to the Europeans rather than press hard for them—little tends to happen.

Finally, leadership—being an effective sheriff if you will—requires that we do at least as much as anyone in the posse. The Gulf War offers something of a model in this regard. We cannot expect to lead if we are not prepared to participate. And we will not be able to participate if we lack the means. Foreign policy depends on using tools wisely, but we cannot use tools we do not have. To deal with the age of deregulation, to regulate an inherently disorderly era, the United States must equip itself for the task.

Equipping ourselves, though, is a matter of both capability and will. We will come to possess the tools only if we build support at home for spending the necessary resources; just as important, we will be able to use the tools only if there is public and congressional support to do so. Domestic support never simply materializes but requires sustained effort by the president and senior executive branch officials and others in positions of authority. Consultations with allies must be complemented by consultations with Congress, just as private diplomacy abroad must be complemented by public diplomacy at home. Absent such an effort to explain why foreign policy still matters and why we cannot afford to ignore it, the domestic foundation on which national security inevitably rests will crumble.

NOTES

1. See Craig Johnstone, "Foreign Policy on the Cheap: You Get What You Pay for," U.S. Department of State Dispatch 6, no. 42 (October 16, 1995), 743–45.
2. "The International Affairs Budget—A Sound Investment in Global Leadership: Questions and Answers," U.S. Department of State Dispatch 6, no. 42 (October 16, 1995), 746–49.
3. Some 60 retired generals and admirals from the United States and more than a dozen other countries released a statement on December 4, 1996, calling for the reduction and then abolition of nuclear weapons. For criticism see Stephen Rosenfeld, "Nuclear Abolitionism," Washington Post, December 6, 1996, A31, and Richard N. Haass, "It's Dangerous to Disarm," New York Times, December 11, 1996, A27.

4. One defense of the single half-war approach is Michael E. O'Hanlon, *The Art of War in the Age of Force: U.S. Military Posture for the Post–Cold War World* (Westport, Conn.: Praeger, 1992). For the opposing perspective, see Charles S. Robb, "Be Ready for Two Desert Storms," *Washington Post*, January 15, 1997, A19. The one versus two half-war debate is thoughtfully discussed in Richard K. Betts, *Military Readiness: Concepts, Choices, Consequences* (Washington, D.C.: Brookings, 1995), 204–09. For a useful overview of the defense spending debate, see Paul K. Davis (ed.), *New Challenges for Defense Planning: Rethinking How Much Is Enough* (Santa Monica, Cal.: Rand, 1994).

5. Much of this discussion of intelligence is drawn from *Making Intelligence Smarter: The Future of U.S. Intelligence* (New York: Council on Foreign Relations, 1996).

6. For background, see *Enhancing U.S. Security Through Foreign Aid* (Washington, D.C.: Congressional Budget Office, 1994), and *Financing American Leadership: Protecting American Interests and Promoting American Values* (Washington, D.C.: Brookings and the Council on Foreign Relations, 1997).

7. See Philip Zelikow and Condoleezza Rice, *Germany Unified and Europe Transformed: A Study in Statecraft* (Cambridge, Mass.: Harvard University Press, 1995).

8. For a more detailed discussion of issues relating to the military tool, see Richard N. Haass, *Intervention: The Use of American Military Force in the Post–Cold War World* (Washington, D.C.: Carnegie Endowment for International Peace, 1994).

9. See Eric V. Larson, *Casualties and Consensus: The Historical Role of Casualties in Domestic Support for U.S. Military Operations* (Santa Monica, Cal.: Rand, 1996). Also see Edward N. Luttwak, "A Post-Heroic Military Policy," *Foreign Affairs* 75, no. 4 (July–August 1996), 33–44.

10. See Michael O'Hanlon and Carol Graham, *A Half Penny on the Federal Dollar: The Future of U.S. Foreign Aid* (Washington, D.C.: Brookings, 1997).

11. For two different but comprehensive sets of proposals on what to do about aid, see Nicholas Eberstadt, *Foreign Aid and the American Purpose* (Washington, D.C.: American Enterprise Institute, 1988), and David Gordon, Catherine Gwin, and Steven W. Sinding, *What Future for Aid?* (Washington, D.C.: Overseas Development Council and the Henry L. Stimson Center, 1996).

12. A useful discussion of the considerations that need to go into choosing a policy can be found in Franklin L. Lavin, "Asphyxiation or Oxygen? The Sanctions Dilemma," *Foreign Policy*, no. 104 (Fall 1996), 139–53.

13. The American debate over China policy is fast emerging as one of the most important and intense of the post–Cold War period. See, for example, Robert Kagan, "What China Knows That We Don't: The Case for Containment," *Weekly Standard* (January 20, 1997), 22–27; Robert B. Zoellick, "China: What Engagement Means," *National Interest*, no. 46 (Winter 1996/97), 13–22; James Shinn (ed.), *Weaving the Net: Conditional Engagement with China* (New York: Council on Foreign Relations, 1996); and Richard Bernstein and Ross H. Munro, *The Coming Conflict with China* (New York: Knopf, 1997).

14. Excerpts of the November 1995 National Intelligence Estimate that assessed emerging missile threats to the United States were printed in the *Washington Times*, May 14, 1996, A15.

15. The debate over ballistic missile defense has been intense. For one exchange, see "Do We Need a Missile Defense?" *Wall Street Journal*, June 20, 1996, A18. For a skeptical view, see Joseph Cirincione and Frank von Hippel (eds.), *The Last 15 Minutes: Ballistic Missile Defense in Perspective* (Washington, D.C.: Coalition to Reduce Nuclear Dangers, 1996). A supportive stance is in *Defending America: Ending America's Vulnerability to Ballistic Missiles* (Washington, D.C.: Heritage Foundation, 1996).

16. For discussion of this issue, see John Gerard Ruggie, "Consolidating the European Pillar: The Key to NATO's Future," *Washington Quarterly* 20, no. 1 (Winter 1997), 109–24.

17. On the question of retaliation in kind and strategic conventional options, see Eric Schmitt, "Head of Nuclear Forces Plans for a New World," *New York Times*, February 25, 1993, B7.

18. For background, see *Ballistic Missile Defense: Evolution and Current Issues* (Washington, D.C.: U.S. General Accounting Office, July 1993), esp. 43–49. In addition, the March 1997 Helsinski summit appears to have gone a long way toward bridging the U.S.-Russian differences over theater ballistic missiles.

19. Amitai Etzioni, "The Evils of Self-Determination," *Foreign Policy*, no. 89 (Winter 1992–93), 21–35.

20. For varying perspectives on this point, see Charles William Maynes, "Containing Ethnic Conflict," *Foreign Policy*, no. 90 (Spring 1993), 3–21; Michael Lind, "In Defense of Liberal Nationalism," *Foreign Affairs* 73, no. 3 (May–June 1994), 87–99; and Radha Kumar, "The Troubled History of Partition," *Foreign Affairs* 76, no. 1 (January–February 1997), 22–34.

21. Robert Cooper and Mats Berdal, "Outside Intervention in Ethnic Conflicts," *Survival* 35, no. 1 (Spring 1993), 139.

22. See U.S. Bureau for International Narcotics and Law Enforcement Affairs, *International Narcotics Control Strategy Report* (Washington, D.C.: Department of State, March 1996) and Paul B. Stares, *Global Habit: The Drug Problem in a Borderless World* (Washington, D.C.: Brookings, 1996).

23. For two powerful critiques of U.S. policy in this area, see Mathea Falco, "U.S. Drug Policy: Addicted to Failure," *Foreign Policy*, no. 102 (Spring 1996), 120–133, and Eva Bertram, Morris Blachman, Kenneth Sharpe, and Peter Andreas, *Drug War Politics: The Price of Denial* (Berkeley, Cal.: University of California Press, 1996).

24. For background, see *United States Dependence on Foreign Oil*, Hearing Before the Committee on Foreign Relations, United States Senate (Washington, D.C.: U.S. Government Printing Office, 1995).

25. Additional revenues could be saved by eliminating as separate agencies the Agency for International Development, the Arms Control and Disarmament Agency, and the U.S. Information Agency.

Conclusion

It is in the interest of the American people to adopt and support a foreign policy of regulation to manage the challenges and exploit the opportunities generated by the post–Cold War world. Alas, this is much easier advocated than realized. A clear and growing gap exists between the demands of implementing a foreign policy of regulation and the will and ability of the United States to meet these demands.

This gap manifests itself in a number of ways, above all in declining resource levels for national security. Spending on defense, diplomacy, and assistance is down considerably over the past decade. Moreover, resource reductions can be seen in other areas: in time devoted to overseas stories by the media, in programs and projects funded by foundations, in offerings by university departments. If nothing is done, downward trends will continue, and current levels of effort, however inadequate, will begin to look high in comparison.

The gap also manifests itself in what we and our leaders are no longer talking about. The year 1992 saw the Bush administration shy away from foreign policy for fear of being branded as out of touch with the "real" concerns of the American people. What was done reluctantly by President Bush and those around him was embraced by candidate Bill Clinton, who ran a campaign that promised a return to economic and social matters.

Once in office, President Clinton devoted the lion's share of his time and energy to domestic issues. Indeed, his has been more of a domestic presidency than that of any of his predecessors since the early Roosevelt era. The 1994 Republican takeover of Congress was similarly based on domestic issues; the Republican "Contract with America" barely mentioned foreign policy. This pattern of essentially paying little attention to foreign policy was repeated in the 1996 campaign. At the same time, Patrick Buchanan, the principal challenger to Republican presidential nominee Bob Dole, advocated a foreign policy that was equal parts isolationist and protectionist. The bottom line was that the American people cared little about foreign affairs, and their elected representatives determined that it made sense to reflect rather than resist this tendency.

This retrenchment in American involvement in the world has not taken place in a vacuum. To the contrary, it is happening at the same time the post–Cold War world is taking shape. What is emerging is a more complicated world in which states increasingly share the stage with other forces and actors, of more powerful weapons in more numerous hands, and of democracies and markets competing with the pull of nationalism and protectionism. It is a world in which American primacy is a fact, but also a world in which the trend away from American preeminence is no less clear.

How, then, is the United States to bridge the gap between the demands of regulating a deregulated world and a society reluctant to play the role of sheriff?

It is a difficult but feasible undertaking. Moreover, it should be done and it can be done in a manner fully consistent with the requirement to put our domestic house in order. Three things are required, however. First, there must be some narrowing of national security goals. The United States cannot make hegemony an aim of foreign policy; hegemony is simply beyond our means. Nor can we hope to save every failed state, settle every civil war, or resolve every conflict. The country must discriminate—not all interests are of equal value, not all threats or problems are of equal import, not all situations have the same potential to be fixed by American intervention—and tailor its actions so that costs do not outweigh the stakes.

Second, the United States needs to develop a new approach to leadership that matches the nature of the age. Alliances made sense in a relatively predictable world in which a common threat provided the necessary impetus and cohesion for formal, permanent groupings. Now the world is anything but predictable and there is no overarching threat. Alliances can contribute but cannot be the central mechanism for dealing with the world.

In some instances, international institutions can become critical. This applies most to the realms of economics and so-called new issues: the environment, health, refugees, and so on. Less realistic, though, is to turn to multilateral organizations for the role of using military force in any but the most limited situations. Such organizations simply lack the requisite consensus and means to act in demanding circumstances. Depending on them would be tantamount to accepting inaction.

Equally unrealistic is a foreign policy predicated on the United States going it alone. Unilateralism rarely proves viable, given U.S. domestic realities and a global situation in which America's ability to have its own way will diminish. Power has spread too much for this, and the United States is too dependent on others. We need allies if not alliances.

What will be required in many instances is for the United States to act as a sheriff, forging posses to deal with problems as they emerge. The composition of such coalitions will vary from situation to situation, as will the purpose and even authority; what will be constant is the requirement for American leadership and participation from states and actors willing and able to contribute in some form.

Third, the United States can be an effective sheriff only if it has the means. The means or instruments must consist of sufficient military force, intelligence, funds for assistance, and diplomatic assets so that the United States can act or empower others to act.

Possession of means, while necessary, is not sufficient. There must be as well the will to employ our assets and enough political power to sustain any such employment when unexpected difficulties and costs arise. A sheriff needs to be more than a bystander. He must be willing to take part and see the effort through if he is to be persuasive and effective. Reliability is essential if other parties are to work with us rather than against us or strike out on their own.

Carrying out such a role will require the overcoming of domestic political resistance. The reluctance to spend and act on behalf of foreign policy when no overwhelming threat is apparent may be characteristic of democracies and even understandable. But it is no less shortsighted and dangerous for being so. That perspective can be overcome only by citizens and political leaders making the case for a foreign policy that is primarily about interests but also embraces values—and that is sober about threats, that is realistic in its aims, and that shares burdens with others.

In short, to lead abroad, a sheriff must first overcome reticence at home. One form of leadership thus requires another. Though rallying the country to meet a clear and present danger is no mean feat, it is not enough. The true test of a leader in a democracy is to rally the people and their representatives behind a mission when the need is not yet clear. This is the test posed by the age of deregulation, which Americans must pass if we are not to squander the spoils of victory in the Cold War.

Acknowledgments

I expect there are many worthy definitions of what makes for a true friend. Let me give you mine: someone who is willing to devote the considerable time and effort required to read and comment on a draft manuscript. Here, then, are some true friends: Michael Armacost, Richard Betts, Gretchen Crosby, Lynne Davidson, Leslie Gelb, Alexander George, Miles Kahler, Gideon Rose, Robert Scalapino, Elizabeth Sherwood, Fred Starr, Bruce Stokes, Fareed Zakaria, and Robert Zoellick. They are a distinguished crew, and I am beholden to them. It is up to readers to decide whether the product is good. What is not open to question, though, is that what I have produced is much better for the suggestions and criticisms I received.

As any author knows, a book also requires the assistance of a good many others. I began this book while at the Council on Foreign Relations and completed it here at Brookings. At the former, I would like to thank Michael Weber in the Publications office and Edward Cone, the copyeditor. There is also Mary Richards, who was with me at the Council and moved with me to Brookings. Mary has commented on and reviewed every page of every draft and has been relentless in her pursuit of books and articles I needed.

Two gentlemen deserve special acknowledgment. The first is Council President (and my good friend) Les Gelb, who encouraged this book from the outset and never despaired when I got sidetracked. Mike Armacost took up where Les left off and urged me to complete the manuscript, even as I was coping with the demands of my new job. The fact that this volume is a Council on Foreign Relations book distributed by Brookings Institution Press could not be more appropriate.

Thanks are also due Jim Hoge and Owen Harries. Parts of Chapter 3 first appeared in the January/February 1995 issue of *Foreign Affairs*; an earlier version of Chapter 4 first appeared in the Fall 1995 issue of *National Interest*. I appreciate their encouraging me to develop my thinking in the pages of their respective (and respected) journals and for permitting me to draw on some of what I wrote for them for this book.

I also want to acknowledge publicly the support of the John M. Olin Foundation. Its generosity and commitment made this book possible.

One item remains: the matter of dedication. I dedicated previous books to my parents, Irving and Marcella Haass, my wife, Susan, and my son, Sam. This one belongs to my daughter, Francesca. In the memorable words of the renowned international relations theorist Maurice Chevalier, thank heaven for little girls.

Index